Brady plays the blues

Brady plays the blues
My diary of the season
Karren **Brady**

PAVILION

Thank you to all Blues supporters who have made my stay at St Andrews the greatest time of my life. This book is dedicated to each and every one of you.

First published in Great Britain in 1995 by
Pavilion Books Limited
26 Upper Ground
London SE1 9PD

Text copyright © by Karren Brady

The right of Karren Brady to be identified
as the Author of this work
has been asserted in accordance with the
Copyright, Designs and Patents Act 1988

Designed by Cole design unit

A CIP catalogue record for this book is
available from the British Library

ISBN 1-85793-657-4

Typeset in Stempel Garamond with
Frutiger by Servis Filmsetting Ltd
Printed and bound in Great Britain by
Hartnolls

2 4 6 8 10 9 7 5 3 1

This book may be ordered by post direct
from the publisher. Please contact the
Marketing Department. But try your
bookshop first.

Chapter 1

a trip to the Orient

What I'd really like to do
is go out there and
wring a few necks

It is 4.45 p.m. and the rest of my weekend centres around how quickly this man in black blows his whistle. I can see Barry Fry going mad on the touchline, shouting, screaming, waving his arms about. He, too, recognizes what a shambles this is. Just another minute and there it goes: Leyton Orient 2 Birmingham City 1. Time to go downstairs and make pleasant chit-chat. At least I've got a cup of tea waiting for me. I look over at our fans, what have they got to look forward to? Herded back to the station, the long journey back to Birmingham, and we lost. We lost! I still can't believe it. Are we in for a whole season of this? What a frightening thought.

I get up from my seat in the directors' box and slouch downstairs to the boardroom. A cup of tea? Oh, very nice, thank you. Yes, well done, well played, jolly good show, you deserved it, no, really. What

KARREN BRADY

I'd really like to do is go out there and wring a few necks. At least Barry can aim his tea cup against the wall.

I've felt like screaming often enough in the last three weeks. Preseason has been a nightmare from the moment the players reported back for training. I should have felt so confident about today and all I could sense was impending doom. We've done so much here since David Sullivan and the Gold brothers took over, but the way we went into this season was like the bad old days again. We got what we deserved, beaten by Leyton Orient – our first defeat of the season, and the way we are going it won't be our last.

And it's my fault. I'm the boss. This one is down to you, Karren. At this exact moment I couldn't feel worse. I'm blaming everyone but myself. The bottom line is if Barry fouls up this season it is as much my responsibility as his. At this rate I'll be ninety and still working at this club. I said I would get David and the Golds their money back and, from where I'm standing, that promise looks as valid as the one about the cheque being in the post. I'll end up as some bent-over grey-haired old crone, hobbling across the pitch at St Andrews. 'I'm not leaving here until David Sullivan and the Golds have got their money back. We're only eight million quid short now.' Their dream is to put Birmingham in the top six of the Premiership, mine is to put £8 million in the bank. Except we played like we didn't deserve to be in the Second Division today and, as for the £8 million, I'd need to turn over the Abbey National in the Bull Ring.

If Barry can't get it right our hands are tied. I don't want to go through FA tribunals again, or sift through countless applications. Let's hope he gets it right. I've got to have confidence in him. Barry has bought most of the squad of forty. They are his players, his 'lads' – if he can't get the best out of them, who can? Time is not on our side. We can't afford to stay two seasons in this Division, not with the money we've put in. If we can't turn this round we might as well give up – we need promotion this season or forget it.

Not a cheerful thought. The performance today was dreadful, little less than disgraceful. Orient's whole team cost roughly our monthly wage bill to assemble, yet they outplayed us, outfought us, they were even more skilful. It seemed we had no pattern, no spirit, no fight.

Suffice to say, I am not on Barry's Christmas card list at the moment. He thinks I poke my nose in too much and that I try to get involved in the football side of running Birmingham City. I don't care, I only interfere when I think I need to, and I will always put what I think is best for the club before any personal popularity contest. For what it's worth, in my opinion Barry should never have been left alone to organize our pre-season friendlies. Maybe the reason we were so poor against Orient today was because we haven't played enough quality sides.

That is why we seem to have fallen out. Last season, Birmingham made in excess of £100,000 from pre-season games. Last year we rang a whole list of contacts at Premiership clubs. By the end of the day, we had Liverpool guaranteed, Norwich arranged, pre-season worked well and it made us a lot of money. Admittedly, this year had to be different because our ground was closed for redevelopment, so where was the cash going to come from? My view was we are a big club, with big support away from home and we should have no problem visiting a few of the more prestigious sides. Except, by this time, the season was drawing nearer and Barry hadn't even mentioned friendly games. So I brought it up, I suggested a return to Liverpool, where we played for a trophy last season, and he hit the roof.

'I'm doing pre-season,' he told me – and I backed off. He then phoned David Sullivan. 'All managers do pre-season and I've never had anyone take pre-season off me in the past.' So then David is on to me.

11

'You can't step on the Manager's toes, you've got to let him do it, you must let him get on with his business.'

I can still remember the look on David Sullivan's face when he saw that we had only earned £10,000 from the pre-season. Suddenly, our previous conversation was forgotten.

'Why didn't you do pre-season?' he shouted. 'Why didn't you put your foot down and tell him?'

'Because you told me not to interfere,' I replied.

In the end, I was glad I left it to Barry, though. Had I arranged pre-season it would now be my fault that we'd just lost to Leyton Orient. In the end I have to keep my cool and let him get on with it.

It seems I've been at loggerheads with Barry over most things lately. Terry Cooper's style and Barry's style couldn't be more different. Terry was tougher with the players than I have ever been, whereas Barry talks a hard game but remains friends with the players. The players wouldn't breath without asking permission from Terry and when he spoke to them, he had the attitude that if they didn't like it they could get lost. Barry's method is to use me as the Hard Guy. He phones and says he is sending a certain player in who wants a rise. I've sat in rooms listening to Barry telling players: 'What can I do, my hands are tied, it's up to Karren and if she won't pay you that money it's not my fault.' And I have to sit there nodding my head like a hard-faced bitch. It means I have no rapport with the players anymore. How can I refuse a wage rise one day, then ask after their wife and kids the next?

Terry tried a trick like this on me once, although he wasn't as cute as Barry. He was signing a player and I told him before negotiations began that the most we would pay was £750 a week basic wage with £10,000 annual signing-on fee. So the player troops in, Terry sits on the desk and I'm sitting behind it and Terry winks at me secretly and says:

'We might be able to get you £850-a-week with a £15,000 annual signing-on fee.'

I said: 'I don't know what you are winking at me for, its £750 and ten grand, take it or leave it.' And the player said: 'OK, I'll take it,' and that was that.

The way it is at the moment, I've had players ringing me up saying: 'My car has broken down, what should I do?' Do what any of us have to do, mate – get it fixed. I get everyone's problems. In fact, it became so bad I raised the matter at a board meeting. I told them I was sick of the players coming to me about every trivial thing and that we should have a procedure where they went to Barry then, if it was outside his area, he came to me. I didn't want another player marching into my office, plonking himself down and saying: 'Right, how much am I getting?'

Barry and everyone agreed this was sensible. Barry would deal with the players, I would work with Barry; and I sent out a memo saying even contract matters had to be taken to the Manager and should be resolved only with him. But again, the very next day, after training, Barry very cleverly sticks his head around the door and says: 'Louie Donowa will be popping in to see you about a new contract later, OK?' I could have strangled him.

Sometimes, though, his style can be pretty devious. Like the time we had to deal with a player signed at a time when I was away from the club and his contract was, for that reason, not the standard one issued to all players. The usual agreement is that we pay for accommodation at the Pineways Hotel for three months until the players have found somewhere to live in or around Birmingham. But this player had a specific clause inserted into his contract saying we would pay for his accommodation until his house was sold, which David Sullivan says he took to mean the house was in the process of being sold.

But there was obviously a problem because nine months down the line the player's hotel bills kept coming in. So I told Barry I needed to speak to him. The player's house, it transpired, hadn't been sold for a very good reason – it hadn't been built! We were meant to put him up in a hotel until he built his own house, then wait for him to sell it and then he would finally move out of paid-for accommodation and into a place he had found near Birmingham. 'That is not in the spirit of our agreement,' I said as firmly as I could to the player. But he continued to insist the club were well aware of his unusual sleeping arrangements. I couldn't see how anyone at Birmingham would have signed a contract potentially lumbering us with hotel bills until it expired – which was three years later.

'Anyway, the inference surely was that your house was on the market,' I added. 'There is no way the club will foot the bills past the next two months. Come up with a compromise: four weeks more or six or whatever you think is fair. Talk it over with your wife and I'll see you next week.'

'I could take you to the Professional Footballers' Association,' the player said.

'I know,' I replied, 'but I'm sure we can work it out between us. See you next week.'

The second meeting took place as planned, but this time Barry was present. The player opened by saying he had spoken to his wife and, no, he couldn't compromise. It wasn't the news I was waiting to hear. I explained patiently that I didn't think it was fair for him to maintain his stance and, technically, it meant we could have to pay his hotel bills for three years, if that is how long it took his house to be built. I told him I didn't think this was made clear at the time the contract was signed and that had it been, we would never have agreed under those terms. Then the conversation turned in a wholly unexpected direction.

'Is this a personal thing?' asked the player. The question took me completely by surprise.

'Of course it's not a personal thing,' I said. 'We've hardly ever spoken before, how can it be a personal thing?'

'Well, I think it's personal,' said the player, and an uncomfortable silence grew in the room. It was then that Barry decided to intervene.

'I believe in telling the truth,' he exclaimed, not altogether correctly as I then found out. 'It is personal.' He turned to the player with a look of total sincerity. 'David Sullivan thinks you're fucking useless, son, and he wants you out as soon as possible.' I looked on in total disbelief, as the player's face changed from shock to abject misery and he looked as if he was going to start crying. That was it, all hell broke loose and I was reaching for hankies for the player.

'That's a lie, Barry,' I said.

'No, no, no,' he insisted, 'let's tell the truth.'

'But, hang on,' I said, 'that's not true. He might have said the team was fucking useless after a bad game, I might have said the team was useless and, if you were at all honest, you have said it at times as well. There have been matches when the team has been crap. But David has never pinpointed individuals and said he's no good and this one's rubbish. That is wrong and you should tell the player it's wrong.'

Meanwhile, the player is pacing up and down my office saying: 'He wants me out, he wants me out,' until Barry finally says: 'Yeah, OK, I made a mistake.' By that time, I'm at my wits end. 'Have the accommodation,' I told the player. 'Come and see me in three months and we'll have another talk.' I didn't want to give in but the player was a first-teamer and I could do without upsetting him and his performance so early in the season. Eventually, the player left, order was restored and I turned to Barry and said: 'I can't believe you did that.'

'Yeah, Kazza,' he said. 'It was a bit of a kick in the bollocks, wasn't it?'

Even if David had told him that the player was useless, wouldn't that conversation have been better kept private, rather than immediately sharing it with the player? Things can get said in the heat of the moment, why hurt somebody's feelings like that? Particularly if you need to get a performance out of them for Birmingham City. In retrospect, though, it was not a half bad move on Barry's part.

The board has already told Barry we must be in the top three by Christmas if he is to stay in the job. That might seem harsh, but I think it actually takes some of the pressure off him rather than the other way around. When a club as big as Birmingham with money invested in them drops into Division Two, it is very obvious they must return as quickly as possible. Barry is a clever manager, so he must have known the stakes would be high. By setting a target for Christmas we made it known that he would not be sacked immediately if we had a slow start. At least he now has something to aim at. This way, it is all out in the open. He has until December to show us he can take us back to Division One. By then we should know a lot more about the future of Birmingham City.

Back to that first match. I look over at David Sullivan who is sitting in the corner of the Leyton Orient boardroom watching the other results roll in and no doubt wondering what's happened. Our first thought was Peterborough, but I could hardly see myself moving up there from London. At least Birmingham is a city – at least it has a bit of potential. Poor David. Looking at him now I wonder what I have got him into. He actually believed winning the Second Division was going to be quite easy – the way he was talking when the season began I think he expected to stroll through every match. A first day defeat at Leyton Orient was not in the script. Not for a moment. I go over to chat with David and glibly tell him that we would get better. I wish there was someone to tell me the same, all I can feel are butterflies and I wonder whether the rest of the board have the same doubts as me. But, for the moment the party line is, don't panic.

In comes Barry. He doesn't look at all well. I suppose in one way it is positive that he should be so downhearted about the performance. It is the only glimmer of hope we have.

It wasn't just that we lost, I can handle a defeat – after all, I've seen enough of them. I've seen us play really well and lose and have gone home happy, looking forward to the next game. But this was bad, so bad. If this is as good as it gets then I can't see anyone at Birmingham still being in a job at the end of the season.

I'm looking at Barry chatting. Maybe this is too big for him. A bigger club, bigger structure, bigger players, maybe he's made that step up and the luck hasn't gone with him. I hope he proves me wrong. We've given Barry till Christmas and we'll stick to that whatever.

I know I am still trying to read Barry, still trying to work him out. We have such totally different styles and personalities, I suppose we have been on a collision course since day one. Still he was my man and I am going to stick by him. I can't see him changing his approach now, not after it was so successful at Southend and Barnet. We're just going to have to learn to live with each other. Or call the whole thing off.

Chapter **2**

mess o'the blues

If this is as good as it gets
then I can't see anyone at
Birmingham still being in a
job at the end of the season

Right, that's it. This morning I have advertised for a new manager but, sadly, he is only to run the club shop. I must confess there have been times in the last four weeks when I have wished I had the guts to go the whole hog and I am beginning to wonder if we did the right thing by making Barry fireproof until Christmas. I think he's taking the piss out of me sometimes. I cheerfully asked the man in charge what his team was before an important Cup tie and he replied: 'Fuck knows!'

Leyton Orient, the team that outplayed us and won 2-1 on the opening day of the season, have gone out and lost their next game 4-0 to Barnet. On the back of our early results season ticket sales have dropped and the first defeat alone cost us around £40,000 over the next two matches. We scraped through in the Coca-Cola Cup after losing our first game to Shrewsbury and League results have been consistently inconsistent. I shudder to think what would have happened had we gone out of the Cup. The financial effects of such an early exit would have been disastrous enough – let alone the harm it would have done to morale. Yet now we have drawn Blackburn in the next round, so maybe some of Barry's luck is returning. Not that I have high hopes of progressing much further. The way we have been playing against some Second Division sides, heaven help us against Blackburn.

This month looks like being as fraught as the last and it is not being helped by the worsening relationship between the board and Barry. One minute they are on honeymoon, the next in the divorce courts and it is doing the club no good at all. When we played Plymouth on 3 September, David wrote in the programme that he was as fed up as the supporters were with our indifferent start to the season. Barry provided the perfect answer, a 4-2 home win, but then went dashing into print himself, saying at the press conference that David didn't know the difference between a goal line and a clothes line. So, the next day, the papers are not full of our best result of the season, but the rift between the Manager and President of Birmingham City. David has put £8 million into the club and is surely entitled to his say. Every fan can talk, every armchair critic, newspaper columnist, even people who haven't paid a penny to watch Birmingham in their lives. So why not the man who rescued the club from extinction? Without David Sullivan and the Golds (David's partners on the board) there wouldn't *be* a Birmingham City, so clearly he deserves to voice his opinion. Football people often have this hypersensitive attitude towards those in the boardroom. The slightest criticism and we are told: 'Football is our business – keep your noses out.' Well, excuse me, but if we have put all the bloody money in, I'd say it was our business too. We are not going to sit around meekly while our money goes up the wall. If we published all the directors' views about the way we have played this season, we would have to sell the official programme off the top shelf at newsagents.

The reality is, the only people getting hurt are the supporters who must be wondering what the hell is going on at the club. It doesn't matter what David thinks, or what Barry thinks about what David thinks. What matters is that we get out of the Second Division as soon as possible, and we are never going to do that while getting constantly sidetracked by petty squabbles that have been blown out of proportion.

After Plymouth Barry has been allowed to take Gary Bull on loan from his old club Nottingham Forest, who was brought in to play last night's game against Rotherham. It certainly has been an education being in Division Two – I didn't even know Rotherham had a football team until we pitched up there. A brief description of the game: crap. The general consensus: woeful, disgraceful, pathetic, desperate, unbearable. I would stick up for the players on this occasion, though. The essence of any team is the management staff, just as it is in business. Whether you work in an office or on a football field, what you do ninety per cent of the time reflects the abilities of the person motivating you.

In short, I am really getting fed up. We cannot seem to find players capable of fitting together, yet all we seem to do is throw more money at the problem. We have forty-two professionals and I know clubs who believe they are overstaffed with ten less than that. As I sit in my office the day after our draw at Rotherham, we are about to buy two more. But David is so desperate to see progress he wants to improve the team immediately. We are buying the players from one of Barry's old clubs, Southend – Gary Poole and Jonathan Hunt – and we are offering Harry Willis and David Regis plus £120,000 in return. I do not think we should continue buying new players and have told David so, but he does not intend to see us flagging mid-table and, in the circumstances, we have to put our trust in Barry. I just think we are being very short-sighted in our outlook.

David Sullivan thinks we are putting Barry under tremendous

pressure to get it right. That may be true, but he has money to wheel and deal and gates that are the envy of all our rivals. Real pressure is trying to succeed with eighteen professionals and crowds of two thousand, as some managers are forced to in the Second Division. We are the big fish in this small pool which is why Barry came here when his old club Southend were better placed in the League. Even when things go wrong as they have done in this first month, Barry does not get grief – he gets more transfer market cash.

But then there is pressure all through the club. The ticket office, for instance, had a disaster with the season tickets last month. No wonder I am intolerant of Barry's problems, having divided the last week between my own job, sorting out the ticket office and restructuring the commercial department. I worked the same hours as when I first came to the club, except I didn't expect to still be having these problems now. I knew there were going to be some difficulties this season because, like many other clubs, we are redeveloping our ground to comply with the Taylor Report and almost half of St Andrews was going to be unfinished when our League programme began. The police did not help us either, making our first two matches all-ticket despite my constant protests and I was very annoyed at their attitude. But our biggest problem was always going to be the season ticket holders whose seats were in the unfinished part of the ground. We had arranged complimentary tickets elsewhere for them and I had left the ticket office staff in charge – until 19 August when I popped over to see how he was getting on.

Under terrible pressure and with little resources, the scene that greeted me reminded me of the bad old days at Birmingham City. For a minute I thought I had walked in on the aftermath of a robbery – I found wads of cash lying about the place next to piles of tickets. Not only had the complimentary tickets not been sent out, they had not even been sorted out. The office had not been able to cope with two all-ticket matches, but instead of getting in temps or staying late to finish work, they had done their best, getting further and further behind. I rolled up my sleeves and mucked in. It was eleven o'clock at night before we left the ticket office, but the work was not yet done and, sure enough, the next day fans arrived in their hundreds to complain. This summer we spent £100,000 on a new ticket office and £50,000 on a new computer system to run it and, if anything, we are less organized than before. When Saturday came the queues were even longer, we had hundreds of tickets to sell for the Shrewsbury game, plus all our season ticket holders stomping around pissed off. As I finally took my seat twenty minutes into the first half, we scored – it was the only thing I had to smile about all day.

The following Monday we solved the mystery of the ticket office. The seating plan programmed into the computer was not the same as the seating plan in the ground – so we were selling tickets for seats that did not exist. To say I was angry is an understatement. I dealt with any remaining season ticket holders and mailed out their tickets for the next two games. At least the ticket office is now running smoothly. Next stop the club shop.

Here again we seemed to be slipping back into the old practices. We had a club shop with little stock and little variety of stock and the profits reflected this. There and then I reorganized the window display, made better use of what they possessed and ordered more merchandise. Within a week the profits were up. What has so disappointed me is that I thought the place was beginning to run so well compared to when we took over in March 1992. When I first clapped eyes on St Andrews I would never have imagined spending the next few years of my working life there.

To begin with, David wanted to buy a racecourse. I think that was the great love of his life until Birmingham City came along, but racetracks only come up for sale once in a blue moon and there weren't many below £15 million. I can remember we talked about it and then decided football was perhaps a better area commercially, but again the huge expense and limitations of opportunity were a problem. Despite all the speculation, few football clubs with any potential to make money or achieve success come on to the market, and when we started looking, the only takeovers offered were at clubs like Peterborough and Barnet. David has always said I liked the finer things of life and he is right. A house in Peterborough is not one of them. I can remember being genuinely worried when he was expressing a serious interest in the place. It is not the sort of location I had really imagined when I was plotting my career moves, but I managed to bring the debate to a speedy conclusion.

'So where exactly is Peterborough, Dave?' I asked him.

'I don't know,' he replied, so that put an end to that.

The best we were offered was Tottenham. One minute we were purchasing a club which we didn't know the location of, the next we were negotiating for one of the most famous clubs in the world. But David decided it was out of our price range and, in the end, Alan Sugar and Terry Venables stepped in. It would have been wonderful to take over a club as prestigious as Spurs. By that time it was accepted that, if we did pull a deal off anywhere, I would leave Sport newspapers to take charge. I was getting impatient to meet my new challenge but, frustratingly, weeks went by without success. Then, after all the clandestine meetings about Spurs, a very public advertisement in the *Financial Times* changed my life. David Sullivan had seen it. It was not big, but it alerted our interest. 'Football club for sale' it read, with a contact number. We spoke to the agent acting on behalf of the liquidators and after they were satisfied we were genuine they revealed the name of the club as Birmingham City. 'Why don't you go up and have a look?' David said to me, and my career in football began.

I drove up on 1 March and in the car I imagined what it would be like to run a big football club. I had quite a cheery little fantasy going of this glamorous place, this giant football club waiting to be revived by my magic touch. Wrong again. I had never been to Birmingham the city, let alone Birmingham the football club and I can remember my first emotions upon seeing St Andrews as not so much disappointment as disgust. I can remember walking out on to the pitch and feeling as if I had stepped into a time warp. It was as if the twentieth century and progress had gone on around this little island of introspection. You could wipe a finger down a wall and inspect five generations of filthy black dust. No one had applied a coat of paint to anywhere in the ground in thirty-five years. It was grim, it was grey, it was horrible. Inside the stadium the offices were dank and dark – the office I have now used to be a store room, but it was hard to tell the broom cupboards from the boardroom at St Andrews as it used to be. We had told the liquidators to keep it a secret that we were coming up, because we felt the local newspapers would be very much against us buying the club if they heard, so the whole thing was very hush-hush. Our plans were to buy the club, go in and announce it on the day when no one could do anything about it. But, at first sight, Birmingham's chances of being bought by Sport newspapers went from 50:50 to 80:20 against. I was walking around more out of politeness, but then two meetings persuaded me we should get involved. The first was with the Manager, Terry Cooper, who I got on with straight away. The second was with the existing directors, who I quickly realized were running the club at a fraction of its potential.

I sat down with Terry and quickly got down to business. 'How much money do you need to stop Birmingham City being relegated?' I asked. I was expecting a trickster. I was expecting to be told: 'Well, you take over and we'll have a look'. But Terry stared me straight in the eyes and said: '£400,000.' We got on fine from that moment. He told me exactly what the money would be used for, which players would be bought with it, which could be sold, and what the end result would be if we did that. He told me what the good and bad points of the club were, why the club had slid into decline and what he felt could be done to arrest that slide. It was probably the meeting with Terry that gave me the inspiration to recommend buying Birmingham to David. I didn't know much about football, I didn't know how a club should be run, I didn't know how to negotiate a transfer deal, but I knew we would have an honest manager who knew his football. I needed to meet people I felt would be on our side – and Terry struck me as one immediately.

Then it was on to meet Chairman Jack Wiseman and Birmingham's Secretary Alan Jones. Our discussion could not have been more different. I was shown to the boardroom, which had obviously been very fashionable in about 1967. There was a carpet that could only have been designed by a blind alcoholic on acid and flock wallpaper that was so discoloured with age it was turning a shade of beige which was too horrible to even contemplate. They had inherited from God knows where a drinks cabinet dating from the dawn of MFI, but everyone looked too scared to open its doors in case the whole thing fell apart. There was a leather sofa that more or less exactly failed to match everything in the room and two chairs, although one had three legs and the other I was warned about sitting on. Peterborough was looking more inviting by the second.

The crowning glory was Jack's desk. He sat behind it with as much dignity as he could muster given the surroundings and I began giving him a carefully prepared quizzing. The whole scene was weird. I had a large notebook with my questions written down and space left for the answers and figures I thought would be supplied. Big mistake. I left with the same notebook, the same questions – but no answers. So how much does the catering make? An embarrassed shuffling of papers and tapping of pens. Silence. We don't know. So how much does the club shop bring in? Same again. What do the ticket sales make? More head shaking.

Jack Wiseman was a Chairman who didn't know how much the club made (since the books weren't available to him) or how long they could stay afloat.

The only figures I could find painted an unrelenting picture of bad news. I saw purchase ledgers for the club shop, the catering, the merchandising and the programme sales and every one showed a deficit. A quick chat with the general manager-cum-catering manager-cum-chief scout had also yielded little in the way of encouragement. I was becoming exasperated. For God's sake, I said, what about your accountant? Well there is this guy who is a sort of accountant, I was told, but we are not sure that is what he does all the time. It was as if everyone at the club just kept their head down in case they got asked an awkward question or had to face up to a none-too-pleasant truth. There was no structure at all. If there was a problem, it was somebody else's problem and no one got directly involved with it. Suddenly, Jack spoke up. 'I'm seventy years old, you know,' he said, 'and I've been here all on my own and I've been doing my best. I've taken time off from my FA duties and I've been here every day. But I didn't want to make any decision or rush into anything until the new people got here.' By now I had seen and heard enough. As I got up to leave Jack said to me: 'Well, you never know, you might come back here as Madam Chairman.' I don't think he thought for one moment he would see me again. 'Well, you never know,' and I rushed back to London to tell David to buy Birmingham.

After what I had seen a lot of people would have thought I was mad, but my recommendation to David could not have been more positive. 'If we are going to buy a football club,' I told him, 'this is the one it should be.' I knew straight away this was not a small club run to its maximum potential, but a big club run so badly it could only improve. There was great potential, a huge catchment area for supporters and this was something that could really be built up. It wasn't like Barnet where the ground only had a capacity of three thousand – I mean, where can you go from there?

'The place is a mess,' I told David, 'we will literally have to get rid of all the old crap and start from fresh.' It was then he started to get cold feet. 'I don't know,' he told me, 'football clubs are just a black hole for money – I don't think it is right.' But that night I was on the phone to him every ten minutes: 'You do want this, Dave, you do, you do. I'll make it work, whatever money you put in, I'll get back, I'll work all the hours, just let me take this on.' I wanted a new challenge, something different, something exciting, something I could really get my teeth into. I wanted Birmingham City. David was now 60:40 against but still talking of racing. I couldn't see the challenge myself – clip, clop, clip, clop once a week. What do you do the rest of the time? And the people you mixed with were such snobs. They were never going to accept David and why the hell should he change for them? Finally, David said: 'Look I'm dead set against this, but if you really think it is the right thing, we'll do it.'

So then we began negotiating with the liquidators because two settlements had to be made. One to the Kumar brothers for their shares, the other for the loans their businesses had given Birmingham City. Meanwhile, the speculation had gone into overdrive and I was by turns a 'mystery woman' buying Birmingham for my father, or buying it for David Sullivan. It was hard to keep the press at bay while the deal was being done, but to my tremendous relief David brought the negotiations to an end with reasonable haste. 'Tell them this is the offer,' he said. 'It is open for five hours and if they don't want it they can forget it.' Then three hours went by and the liquidators rang back to say we were the new owners of Birmingham City. For me, it was the loveliest feeling in the world. The honeymoon didn't last long, though.

Our first game was at home to Oxford on 6 March. We were in the bottom three and looked certain to go down, yet we got our biggest gate since November and, to my horror, Jack Wiseman made me go out on to the pitch. What followed was even worse. David wanted us to go into the dressing room and introduce ourselves to the players, which I thought was a waste of time. But David said it was important, so in we went. The dressing rooms were as grotty as the rest of the club and we couldn't have got a more dismal reception had we announced we were here to wind the place up. David spoke to the players.

'We're the new owners, we're here to do good things, there are fourteen games left until the end of the season and if we don't start winning we're going to end up in the Second Division. A lot of supporters have turned up for you today, so it is important we start winning. Not just this week, but next week and the week after. You've got to decide where you want to play – the decision is yours and it starts today.'

Nothing – not a word from the players. So David starts again: 'I know you haven't got a proper training ground, I know some of you haven't been paid, but we are going to change that. You won't have to use changing rooms with five hundred people anymore, you won't have to go without bonuses and contracts. We want team spirit, we want you all together so we can get out of this.'

Silence. And I was standing alongside him thinking: 'Holy shit, get me out of here. These people hate us.' I think that was the first time I realized what a strange and intimidating place a football club can be to outsiders. We had come to a club about to be dissolved, a club that would be extinct were it not for our involvement, saved everybody's jobs and no one even said 'welcome'. I was genuinely disappointed. But we did win the game 1-0. And then the real work began.

The first job was to change the strip back to Birmingham's traditional blue and white. The Kumars had added flashes of orange and green – the colours of the Indian flag – all over it. We ordered fourteen

31

new traditional strips for the first-team only and then I went to London to see Arsenal's Vice-Chairman David Dein for some advice on how to run a football club.

David has always been supportive of me. I met him through my dad, Terry, who is a big Arsenal fan and David was the only person I knew with experience of running a football club. We sat and talked for two hours because I needed to close all the black holes as quickly as possible. He told me what we should be making from the catering, what we should be making from our kit deal, who I should go to, who I should speak to, how much programme sales should bring in, what we should expect from merchandising. He told me to ring the clubcall line every day to check that none of the players were slagging off the manager and, before I left for Birmingham, he gave me one last piece of advice: 'You might be a businesswoman now,' he said, 'but the football fever will grip you and you must never let your heart rule your head. You think I'm stupid now, but there will come a time when your heart thinks "one more player" and your brain says "we can't afford it". Go with your brain every time. Tell yourself this every day. It's very important.' And, of course, he was right.

So I travelled back to St Andrews with these big ideas, little realizing how sorely I had underestimated the chaos at the club. The mess I discovered was truly horrific. To begin with, Birmingham City had no cashflow. If they needed anything they had to barter for it. If they ran out of black plastic bags and needed to sweep the terraces, they would exchange an executive box worth £6,000 for a year's supply of bags. If a typewriter broke, they would offer the repair man a season ticket to come and fix it. Even tea and coffee were purchased that way – there was literally no money. Decisions on the most menial purchasing were made at board level because Birmingham's predicament was so desperate. Before we arrived senior executives had sat around discussing whether we should let Electrolux have an advertising hoarding for nothing so we could get our hands on a new vacuum cleaner. No one had the sense to realize it was a vicious circle because bartering meant there was no possibility of bringing in proper commercial revenue. In other departments, people were simply kidding themselves and pretending they were making a profit. When I looked at the accounts for the club programme, I discovered they were including the freebies given to box holders, directors, players and sponsors as part of the sales. They were internally invoicing our own commercial department! It meant we were selling four thousand programmes and giving away another thousand but our ledgers said we had sold five thousand. And we wondered why our books didn't add up! It was pure self-delusion.

I have often been asked what experience I had in running a football club. The answer in none, but businesses are the same the world over. Money comes in, money goes out – all you have to do is make sure the first figure is more than the second. Football club expenses are roughly the same as any other business – wages, VAT, tax, lighting, heating, office costs are no different. Only police costs and transfer fees are exceptional. The problem at Birmingham was that no one knew what these individual costs were – they did not know how much they paid the police, they did not know how much it cost to run the office. So the final equation between incomings and outgoings could never be made.

So I returned to Birmingham, reorganized our catering and managed to wipe out the earlier losses. Then I franchised the club shops for £150,000 plus bonuses so that they could be put into order. We would be able to take the shops back after about a year and run them more efficiently ourselves. Next I turned my attention to the programme. We were employing an editor on £20,000 plus company car, an assistant on £6,000, charging £1 for each programme and 80 pence of that was printing costs. By the time you took the two salaries into account, plus any articles that had to be paid for, the whole thing was losing a fortune. They hadn't even got quotes from two printers – they just went to the first one they found. So I found a cheaper printer, sacked the editor, made his assistant the boss, put the price of the programme up to £1.50 and suddenly we were making a profit.

At the end of the first week I can remember lying in my hotel room at the Hyatt staring at the ceiling and thinking: 'Oh God, I've made a huge mistake.' Even with the strides we had made in seven days there was still so much to be done. We were buying and selling players on a daily basis to reorganize the squad before the transfer deadline, and bailiffs were arriving every two minutes demanding to take stuff away. You never knew what direction they were coming from because there was no list of outstanding bills. In one room someone would be demanding the removal of furniture to the value of £35.27, the next minute a bailiff from another creditor would serve notice of a £10,000 debt. I was trying to ward these people off while asking my staff questions like how many shirts did we sell last year and getting blank looks of incomprehension by way of a reply.

I was answering phones, letting bailiffs in and out, sweeping the terraces and my secretary had a typing speed of one poorly-spelt letter a day. It was impossible to get anything done and, had we remained like that, we would have gone to the wall. There was only one thing for it – I was going to have to sack the staff.

I called a meeting and laid it on the line. I have never been so angry. 'Listen', I said, 'This is the leisure industry and customer service doesn't begin and end with picking up the phone. No one will ever again answer a call, say "nah, I don't deal with tickets" and put it down again. That isn't service. Do that and you're fired.'

But it was no use. Things were not going to change and I had to make a clean sweep. There are only three people remaining from the time we took over, although I can't say I felt sorry for the previous lot. They were doing their jobs so badly getting the sack cannot have come as any great shock. What I couldn't believe is the previous owners had allowed a business to run like that. No one got estimates, no one thought of company expenditure. At the end of the first week I began to think it would be impossible to tie the money down because as soon as I plugged one hole, a new one opened and more cash disappeared down it. Players would come into the office and say: 'Sorry to bother you, but I haven't had my signing-on fee from two months ago.' So I would go to the accounts office and it would be: 'Oh, sorry, I've paid it into the wrong account.' I looked at the sheet and saw the name of a player who had left the club, but was still getting paid. On the first Wednesday, I came into the office and there was a line of players queuing up the stairs after training. 'What's this?' I asked. 'Wages day,' I was told. And we were all expected to queue like that, forming a line and waiting for a clerk to push our cheque through the little window. On match days, the same window acted as Birmingham's only ticket outlet, so you had two thousand people queuing up the stairs instead. It was unworkable. And anyone who sold a ticket had to write their name down and the amount they took. 'Why?' I asked. No one knew. 'It's just the way we do things at Birmingham,' was the most common reply, as if they cracked some marvellous new innovation in business practice. By the end of the first week I was convinced I was not going to cope on my own. I'd done a shirt deal, rearranged the catering, the club shop, the programme, sacked half the staff, took new staff on and we were still nowhere near started. But whenever David phoned I couldn't confide in him because he would have said: 'I told you so.' So I had to keep telling him things were going wonderfully when inside I was thinking, 'Help!' I used to lie awake at night wondering what I was going to do next, how I would handle this, what I would do about that, it was absolutely unbearable. I couldn't go out, I couldn't relax, I existed in two environments – Birmingham City and my hotel room. I got up, I went to work, I came home, I ate steak and chips, I went to bed, I got up, I went to work . . . At the end of those seven days, David told me I had performed a miracle. 'Thanks,' I said, 'and I'm grey for it.' I had to psyche myself up every morning before I went to work: 'Keep going, keep going, it will sort itself out in the end.'

I think the day I knew we would make it was 8 May 1993, when we beat Charlton 1-0 and stayed up. The weeks in the build-up to that have been some of the happiest of my working life. It was like having the worst yacht in the race, but winning through sheer determination. David, the Golds and I were Captains of the boat and the crew were working like mad, there was a great feeling of togetherness and team spirit. Terry Cooper was a nice guy and he only bought nice players, so we had this lovely bunch of lads who believed in themselves and they kept us in the First Division. We have never had that same family atmosphere since and I think Terry appreciated the fact he had been allowed to get rid of a lot of players who had been a problem to him. Most of the team were either Lou Macari's or Dave Mackay's boys and many resented Terry. But the money David put into Birmingham allowed Terry to change his staff, too, and the mood at the club became fabulous. Terry said the players sat around after training and talked, whereas before they just got changed and went home. But I knew none of this would matter if we went down and during that last game I shook with trepidation for ninety minutes. I sat in the director's box making deals with God, giving up smoking, drinking and living like a nun if he would just let us stay up. I'll never forget the moment Paul Moulden scored our winner. It was then I knew all this work would not be in vain.

Everyone said Paul's goal was offside, but we didn't care. I was dancing around like we had won the Cup, so was David and then we all went to the bar to celebrate. Then the funniest thing happened. I was chatting away when this man came up to me and introduced himself as the linesman.

'I gave that goal to your side,' he said, 'and everyone says it's offside.'

'Don't worry about it,' I told him.

'I'm not', he replied. 'I'm retiring today.'

'Get this man a drink,' we shouted, I think the celebrations went on until four in the morning.

If only we had known what the next season held for us.

Chapter **3**

man hungry soccer boss ate my hamster

I knew my relationship with
Paul could mean the end of
my career in football

This morning I am horrified to discover in two-inch high letters in the *Sun* that I am a 'MAN HUNGRY SOCCER BOSS' who 'STOLE MY MAN'. The 'man' is my fiancé (now my husband) Paul Peschisolido and the woman I supposedly 'stole' him from turns out to be his ex-girlfriend Carmen. I get the *Sun* delivered at home, but I hadn't seen it when my dad called at the crack of dawn to inform me of the story. Understandably, I was deeply upset. He read the whole piece over the phone to me and it was as tacky as the headline suggested. What about this quote, for instance? 'She's greedy for men,' stormed Carmen, showing the ring Paul gave her. It is rubbish from start to finish, of course, but these kind of stories can cause more than enough problems for both of us. At best, Pesch can expect an embarrassing ribbing from his team-mates at Stoke, but that's light compared to the abuse he could get from supporters. In the meantime, everyone who has read the story now thinks I am a complete bitch.

I woke Paul up. 'Have you heard this?' I said. 'Your last girlfriend Carmen has stitched us up in the *Sun*.'

'She wasn't my last girlfriend,' he cuts me off. 'I knew her when I was nineteen. I've had about ten girlfriends since then – I haven't seen her in two years.'

Apparently, there was no ring either, so the poor girl is either mad or desperate. Probably both. It amazes me that people want to do things like this when it is so demeaning for everyone involved. It is doubly sad that someone can trot out a pack of lies and have it reported as fact. If anything, Paul was even more upset than I was, yet he had no reason to be. It was not as if he could have done anything to prevent this. The newspaper did not speak to him, me, or anyone who would have knocked this story. I phoned Stuart Higgins, the Editor and a friend of mine. 'I thought we were mates?' I said. 'If I didn't like you, I'd sue you.' What cheesed me off more than anything was that I had never even met the girl. What reason had she to be so nasty to us? She might have been unhappy at splitting up with Paul, but why take it out on us now? But anyone in the public eye has to take some of the more sensational stories with a pinch of salt and forget them, otherwise they end up becoming complete egomaniacs.

In general I have a good relationship with the press – particularly the *Sun*, in fact – but when you get criticized it is easy to fall into the trap of becoming very self-centred about your treatment at the hands of the media. I could end up scouring newspapers for every critical or negative word about me and Birmingham. But anyone who does that is finished. I only blow my top when an article is completely outrageous – but some of the stuff people think is offensive to me, I find ridiculous enough to be amusing. I can remember when Derek Pavis, the Chairman of Notts County, made a fuss about my presence in his boardroom, and Stuart Higgins rang me from his office in Wapping. Pavis had made a comment about 'tarts in the boardroom' and Stuart seemed very worried.

'We've got this headline about you,' he said. 'I want to make sure you won't take offence.'

'What is it?' I asked.

'YOU TART!' he said. Charming. What on earth made him think I would take offence at that?

'Stuart, do what you have to do,' I told him, 'I know it's newsworthy.' Something as far-fetched as that doesn't bother me – in the last two years I have taken a lot worse.

The day we were due at the Football League Commission to decide whether we had illegally poached Barry Fry from Southend, I woke up to another lump of tactful tabloid journalism. On the back page of the *Daily Mirror* was the biggest picture of myself I had ever seen, underneath the headline 'SEX SHOOTER'. The story was sparked by remarks made by Vic Jobson, the Chairman of Southend. He announced that I would be arriving for the meeting like Sharon Stone in *Basic Instinct*, with a short skirt and no knickers to influence the panel. I just couldn't see how my underwear, or lack of it, could become the most important sports story in a national daily newspaper. The whole thing developed into high farce because at one time the Queen's Counsel representing Southend at the hearing quoted David Sullivan from a press report saying: 'Barry Fry is my first choice and I am going to make sure I get him.' 'Well,' I contested, 'the press do tend to exaggerate. For example, I am wearing knickers today whereas the readers of the *Daily Mirror* think I am here flashing my all.'

It was one of the more colourful exchanges of the afternoon and I think that was the day I realized I was becoming a public figure. I had received a fair amount of attention when we first took over Birmingham, but this was different. No matter how much I viewed myself as just another person going to work, the fact was I was a young woman in charge of a football club and I was now in the spotlight. Had I been a middle aged male chief executive of a First Division club, would anyone be the least bit interested in my private life, sleeping arrangements or whether I had Y-fronts on? I think not. I could blend into the background, keep a low profile, do my job and go home. It is not that I mind the extra attention, just that I do get fed up with the trio of cosy pigeon-holes the media have selected for me. I am either a tart chasing after all the young footballers and asking for photographs of Ryan Giggs for my bedroom wall. Or I am a ruthless, domineering bitch, hiring and firing my way through a game I know nothing about. Or I am the Spokesperson for Wimmin of the 1990s – the one the television companies always trot out when they want a quick soundbite on chauvinism in football. 'Is it hard being a woman in a man's world, Karren?' Oh, give me a break. Also, because I am now married to Pesch I have become a target for cynics who suggest it was only a matter of time before I got my claws into one of the players. Nothing could be further from the truth.

The majority of stories about me have been wildly exaggerated. For instance, my bedroom wall is not plastered with photographs of Ryan Giggs, as was suggested in *Private Eye*.

When I had just arrived at St Andrews I was in charge of setting up the match day mascot, who is given a number of mementoes of his day. This particular little boy wanted a signed photograph of Ryan Giggs, but we only had two days to get it. So I phoned the sports desk at the *Sunday Sport* and asked for their help – and when I ask for things to be done, I expect it done straight away. The next week in *Private Eye* there was a story that I stopped production of the *Sport* to get a picture of my hero Ryan Giggs for my boudoir. Someone at the paper had obviously been waiting for years to get at me, and suddenly seized his chance. As a result, I even ended up with a Ryan Giggs duvet cover, courtesy of Frank Skinner and David Baddiel on the *Fantasy Football* television programme!

It fits in with the clichés to imagine that I came to Birmingham, chased after the footballers and landed Pesch. I know what people think, I know what they say, and I knew that when we decided to announce that we were an item it would do me no favours. But I think I have made enough sacrifices in my life and losing Paul would have been one too many. I have given up a lot for my job. Some people can look back at their mad young life, remember trips they took around the world, how they dropped out for a year, how they partied all night at university. I can't. I went to work. And there came a point in my life when I had to choose between my job and me. And this time I chose me.

When I met Paul I was a workaholic. It was not long after we had taken over at St Andrews and I was still in my routine of travelling to my office and back to the Hyatt every day, with no breaks for fun or my social life in the middle. I didn't know anyone in Birmingham, I didn't go anywhere, I didn't do anything. Not exactly *In Bed With Madonna*, more In Bed With My Dinner. I was so desperate to break that routine I offered myself up to make all the personal appearances that go with running a football club. Usually, players are called upon to do them and they hate it but, for me, it was a welcome break from steak and chips for one in my room. Pesch was in the same situation: lonely, on his own in a bed and breakfast, and available to do PAs anywhere because the alternative was watching television. In the end, we started doing quite a lot of things together, supporters' club dos, local talent contests and we got to know each other, becoming quite close friends. Then when he got injured and went into hospital I was in Birmingham doing nothing and went to see him. It all sprang from there and over Christmas two years ago we got together properly.

Having worked twelve hours a day since I came to Birmingham – even on Christmas Day – meeting Paul was the first bit of light relief I had been able to enjoy. He is the nicest person I have ever met, warm and funny and good-looking. When I went on holiday with my mum for a week soon after we started going out together I rang him every day and he was never in. For the first time in my life I found myself wanting to spend more and more time with someone and feeling upset if I couldn't speak to him. Then I knew I loved him. He is very down to earth and normal and doesn't get insecure or envious if I get more attention than him.

The danger of what we were doing made us bond very quickly. We both had a lot at stake and had it been anything less than love staying together just would not have been worth it. I made up my mind to tell David and get it over and done with. I knew my relationship with Paul could mean the end of my career in football. I was not sure how people would perceive me and I was very aware of the need for the whole thing to be handled carefully and sensibly. My first exchanges with David did not bode well.

'The press are following me,' I explained. 'I have done something you might be a bit angry with.'

'Don't worry,' he said, 'nothing can be that bad – it's not as if you have run off with one of the footballers.'

'Ah, well,' I hesitated. 'Actually, I have.'

'Who?'

'Paul Peschisolido.'

'Thank God for that,' he said. 'At least it's not one of Villa's.'

Then I explained what had happened, making sure he knew it wasn't some fly by night thing. David was very supportive. 'You have got your reputation to consider,' he said. 'If this is what you want, then do it. If this isn't what you want, don't. And if you've already done it and he turns out to be a wrong 'un, let's hope he knows how to keep his mouth shut.' Jack Wiseman, too, could not have been kinder. 'Paul is one of the nicest people in the club,' he said. 'Good luck to you both.'

The second most difficult decision was when to go public, but then I got a phone call which made up my mind. It was a reporter from the *People* accusing me of persecuting one of Birmingham's players, as the result of a lovers' tiff. I have been accused of a lot in my life, but knocking off this particular player is about as low as it can go. He moved into a hotel paid for by the club for three months and ran up £400-worth of bar bills, video bills, dry cleaning bills, the works. It was always accepted that extras are paid by the player himself, yet he walked out without settling his account, then complained when we docked the money from his wages. Even Barry had told him he was in the wrong. But, now, according to the *People*, it was a lovers' tiff, an affair that had gone wrong and I was being vindictive. They were doing a story on it, I was warned. 'Oh, do me a favour,' I said. 'I can't stand him – of all the people in the world for me to go to bed with and you pick him.' As soon as I had put the phone down on the *People*, I contacted Paul. 'This can't go on,' I told him. 'The sooner we announce the fact that we are an item the sooner it will all just go away.' So we did. And it didn't. We had reporters camped outside the doorstep, photographers snatching pictures in the street. All because two single people are going out. Is that news?

Even now, I still get hassled over my relationship with Pesch. When he left the club there were suggestions it was because of me and to read the local papers you would think our relationship has been a disastrous influence on his career.

The problems began because Pesch wanted a new contract and a wage increase. My immediate reaction was to hand the whole thing over to David and Barry because, for obvious reasons, it would not be right for me to be involved. Barry's attitude was that Pesch deserved it as our leading goal scorer two seasons running; David thought we should wait until November because Pesch had been injured. Barry gave the club two choices: give him a new contract or sell him now, because he didn't want Pesch to stay at the club unhappy. Eric Hall, the agent, was instructed to see who was interested and we had bids in the region of £500,000 from Notts County and Stoke. The board did not want to sell Pesch that cheaply, but Barry insisted. 'There are problems in the dressing room and I can't cope,' he said. 'The players don't think they can talk around Pesch because he lives with Karren, it has created a bad atmosphere and we've got to sort it out.' Off Pesch went.

Maybe Barry thought he was doing me a favour by getting Pesch a move for more money. But the story had been news since April 1994 – it was a bit of a delayed reaction if it was causing a rift! I told David this but he wouldn't believe me. Barry said there was unrest, and David believed him.

Even now, the local Birmingham paper still finds ways to get at us both over our relationship. Whenever Stoke play in the Midlands area, Paul gets stick from the opposition fans about me. They say certain things, sing certain songs, anyone who has ever been to a football match can imagine their nature. They are no different to the songs and taunts aimed at any striker at any club in the League. No news there, you would think? Not to read the local paper when Stoke played West Brom. In that game Paul's treatment was, apparently, worse than ever and, when he scored, they claimed Pesch had made a certain gesture to the fans taunting him. It wasn't obscene but, even if it was, we could hardly be less bothered. But the following day in the local paper, a whole page was devoted to how poor Paul cracked under the pressure because the songs were about me. It was as if it was my fault! John Evans, the Secretary of West Brom, had tried to be fair and defended Paul by saying he was under a lot of pressure and couldn't be blamed for what he had done, and they turned this round to an attack on me. I felt that the whole tone of the story was that if he didn't know this horrible person he wouldn't have been subjected to this abuse and wouldn't have cracked under the pressure. Yet every player gets abuse whether it is over their girlfriend, their haircut or the size of their nose. And Paul is a big boy well capable of looking after himself without the help of the newspapers. A local paper said we – meaning David Sullivan, the Gold brothers, Barry Fry and myself – should all go back to London because the team had been taken for pre-season fitness training on Dunstable Downs and not to some local hills. They took the whole of the back page over to tell us to get out, ignoring two key issues. Firstly, without these so-called Cockneys they so despise, Birmingham City would have sunk into the mud long ago. Secondly, that their beloved Lickey Hills do not have so much as a changing room near them, and you can't just dump a group of players in the middle of nowhere by coach and tell them to get on with it. What was most hypocritical of all was that Aston Villa had taken their players to Spain to prepare for the season, without so much as a murmur of protest. At least we stayed in England.

I have always found the local press far harder to deal with than the national tabloids. One of their reporters even phoned David to advise him Birmingham City would get better publicity if they sacked me. Quite frankly, it is none of the newspaper's business if David puts Karren Brady or your usual male executive in charge at St Andrews. David told them where to get off, but the next time their reporter saw me he chirped: 'Hello, Karren, how are you?' as if I was some dummy who couldn't see through his smarmy grin. A football club's relationship with the press should be one of mutual support. We want all the publicity we can get, they want to sell as many papers as possible. It makes sense to help each other. Everyone complains about newspapers like the *Sun* but, apart from an isolated incident, I have always found you stand more chance of getting stitched up by the likes of local rags.

About a year into my time at Birmingham a journalist from

KARREN BRADY

another local paper came to interview me. I was very busy at the time with the Football League Commission investigating whether we had poached Barry from Southend and didn't really have the time, but I agreed to do the piece because I thought the local paper could do with our co-operation. I had to cancel our first meeting and then I kept her waiting for twenty minutes while I finished another meeting. I apologized but no sooner had we sat down than the club solicitor Henri Brandman rang about the hearing. 'Would you mind waiting outside, it's a personal call?' I said. We tried again, then there was another call. By that time my proposed interrogator was huffing and puffing like an old steam engine, obviously perturbed at not receiving my undivided attention. Finally, the interview began.

'I bet you're absolutely gutted you didn't buy Villa,' she bitched.
'Why?' I asked.
'Because they're successful and you're not,' she replied.
Now what sort of a question is that? 'Listen,' I told her, 'The only reason I'm doing this is to be helpful to a local newspaper, I'm not on an ego trip here. So if you want to ask questions like that, piss off.' Which she did. I thought the interview ended there, but she still wrote her story, saying how I had gone from being a nice person to a complete bitch, how she had been kept waiting, messed about and was finally told to piss off. I really believe the nationals would not have been that petty.

Basically, as a woman in a high-profile position at a football club you are stereotyped as much, sadly, by other women as the men. Either you have to be completely and utterly feminine and play the role of a glamour puss or you have to be a strident feminist who talks about every issue from a woman's point of view. Both options lead to an equal amount of nonsense. The first undermines your intellect, the second isolates women yet further as curiosities, not real people doing real jobs. I get constantly fed up with being asked to speak 'as a woman' as opposed to a business person, as if my personal opinions can be applied to all women. I am not going to champion the cause of women every time I get the chance. It is not my job, it is boring and it defeats the object. I present a show on Wire TV, a cable station, and one of the producers believed strongly in promoting feminist causes and thought I should, too. When we devoted the show to boxing – one of my favourite sports, incidentally, and one in which I have good contacts – I knew I could call in a few favours and get some famous names on the programme.

'I'm going to get a female boxer,' she said.

'Why,' I asked, 'no one watches women boxing, it's a non-sport and a waste when we could get Chris Eubank.'

'It's another opinion,' she said, 'a very valid one, in fact. How can you say it doesn't matter what women think of boxing?'

'Because no one's interested that's why,' I told her. 'No one gives a stuff what women think about boxing.'

'Unless we give them coverage,' she replied.

My response was: 'This is boring. It's dead. Move on.'

I am not out there to strike a blow for women, I am not flogging my guts out for any other reason other than I love my job. I work because I want to. The only reason I work in football is because it is a damn sight more interesting than almost anything else I can think of. I am not looking to revolutionize football from within, I am looking to do the best job for myself and the club and its directors and shareholders. In a funny way, it has gone full circle, because now I am meant to be a role model for women, whereas when I worked for Sport newspapers I was accused of selling out. It only further confirms my opinion that people should worry about their own lives before they moralize and judge others.

I was in charge of sales and marketing at the *Sunday Sport* and we could only attract very fringe advertising for a period of time so, yes, I was responsible for filling the newspaper with 0898 phonelines. It was a simple financial decision. If we broke the advertising space up into little boxes for sexy phonelines we could make £20,000, if we used the same space to advertise one car firm the rate would be £2,000. As the circulation dropped the advertising revenue became more and more important, so the percentage of sex advertising rose. At the start the split was 50:50 sex and straight, now it is nearer ninety per cent versus ten per cent. I did not have a problem with that then, I do not have a problem with it now. I used to have to read the scripts for the phonelines and they were such twaddle I failed to see why anyone ever bothered to listen to them, let alone get offended or turned on by them. 'Hi, my name is Sandra, and I'm lying on my bed now and if you keep listening I'm going to be telling you what I am doing.' Then, ten minutes of utter drivel later 'I'm wearing my nightie.' The only thing it offended was your intelligence. It wouldn't shock a twelve-year-old. The only thing I can ever remember rejecting was stuff that mentioned urinating on people. Straight sex or titillation I did not see as a problem because seventy-eight per cent of *Sport* readers are male and the product has to be bought.

Even working for a newspaper full of photographs of half-naked models did not bother me. No one is forced to be a glamour model, no one is intimidated to take their clothes off if they don't want to. We got hundreds of submissions and portfolios every week from girls desperate to appear in the *Sunday Sport*. How can someone be exploited if they are making a conscious decision to go down that path? A topless model gets £200 for one hour's work. Some factory workers get £2.50. Now which one do you reckon is being exploited? I've never posed for those pictures myself, but I would never judge someone who did. What right has anyone to decide how another person makes their living? Providing it is legal and no one gets hurt, what is the problem? I get the *Sport* delivered at home every day and I flick through it. No one buys the *Sunday Sport* for serious political discussion or in-depth analysis of the major issues. They buy it because they are more interested in the size of Elle McPherson's nipples than the state of the stock market. It is a raunchy, saucy newspaper and there is a market for it. I would never entertain the notion it is harmful and at one stage it was selling over 600,000 copies with a similar cult following to the adult comic *Viz*. It is funny and lively, glamorous and entertaining.

I can remember walking into rooms at the Advertising Standards Authority with the bigwigs from the other papers and getting no respect. It didn't bother me. We had our market and they had theirs. If you worry what people think about you all the time, you might as well go to work in a bank. I will never be ashamed of my background working for Sport newspapers. Without the money we made at its height, Birmingham City would not have been funded and saved, so it has kept a lot of people in work.

My mum, of course, who is very strait-laced, could never bring herself to tell people where I worked. When asked, she would say: 'Karren works in advertising.' Now she is only too happy to reveal her daughter is the Managing Director at Birmingham City. Funny that – some of the things you hear said about the performance of a losing team wouldn't go amiss on an 0898 number.

Chapter **4**

high noon and
Gary Cooper

Birmingham has become a journalist's dream and this Managing Director's nightmare. Most clubs in our Division can't get in the newspapers; we can't get out of them

Gary Cooper scored the winning goal in the FA Cup draw against Scunthorpe last night. Not big news away from Birmingham City, I'll grant you, but an event with great significance for myself and our management team. Gary's transformation into one of the best players at the football club sums up the way we are all at last beginning to pull in the same direction this season. A few weeks ago he considered signing on the dole rather than playing for us, a few weeks ago we wouldn't have cared if he had; a few weeks ago the Manager and David Sullivan were at loggerheads and results were down the toilet. Now we are a happy, smiling ship for the first time since Barry arrived – and we haven't lost a match since the middle of September.

Of course, it wouldn't be Birmingham without a few squalls during our otherwise tranquil passage. So, for good measure, we've had an attempted coup within the backroom staff, the PFA called in over the disappearance of a player, a huge barney between me and the naked manager outside the dressing room, a televised verbal assault on David Sullivan and a row over signing a new striker. If this was a soap opera it would fail the reality test.

Let's start at the beginning. On 16 September, the day after Harry Willis and Dave Regis were sold to Southend in exchange for Gary Poole and Jonathan Hunt, our most senior first-team member and player-coach Mark Ward contacted David Sullivan. He told him the training was 'mickey mouse' and blamed it for our disappointing start to the season. He wasn't angling for Barry Fry's job. Barry had until December to get us into the top three and had been promised no decision would be made on his future until then, so Mark must have known he had no chance of getting it. But, since Mark was an experienced player, David was keen to listen to his ideas to see if they could be put to any use, so he contacted me and asked what I thought. I said if Mark had any suggestions he should take them up with Barry personally, not with us, and told him to tell Mark exactly that. Problem solved, I thought. Hardly. The next minute Barry came bursting into my office.

'I've had David on,' he raged, 'he says Mark Ward reckons the training is shit.'

'He was only voicing an opinion, Barry,' I said, 'I know he has probably gone about it the wrong way but he was only trying to help.'

'Well, he should have voiced it to me not the fucking owner,' Barry continued. 'Anyway, I don't know how the fuck he knows what goes on in training, he's never there. He's been injured all season. If he's so worried about training, why doesn't he come back in the afternoons to do some extra work with some of the other lads. He doesn't want to do that, does he? He says the players are down about Harry and Dave going – well, I've heard nothing like that. It's nonsense.'

I could see this was going to develop into another Birmingham crisis, so I quickly nipped the player revolt in the bud. 'It is not up to the players to be up or down about who comes and goes, Barry,' I said, 'we make those decisions and you know that. And let's face it, they were hardly the stars of the team. One was here less than a year, the other two months, they weren't even first-team regulars. No one had time to get that attached to them. Now, let's go to training and get Mark Ward and Edwin Stein back and have a good talk about it all and decide who takes training and who is responsible for what. It is no good having the management staff bitching behind each others backs, we'll sort this out straight away.' We both knew a row like this could get out of hand with so many volatile people involved, and the next thing it would be all over the papers unless we acted swiftly.

Barry called to say Edwin had already left for the day but Mark would be in to see me that afternoon. My first thoughts were that Mark would help out more with ball skills as he achieved a high level of skill himself as a player with Everton and West Ham. Edwin would continue to have overall control of all fitness and coaching duties. If we have the talent at the club to make the team better, why not make full use of it? If they shared the duties everyone would stay happy. By the time I met Mark I could see 'happy' was the last word anyone would use to describe our training camp. Barry had rightly bawled him out for taking his problems direct to David Sullivan, while Edwin had called him every name under the sun. Mark claimed it was all a misunderstanding, but I told him he could explain when we had our meeting on Monday.

In the following twenty-four hours, however, it emerged that the relationship between Barry Fry and Mark Ward was the least of our worries. That Sunday we played Peterborough at St Andrews and, for the first time, Pesch sat next to me in our directors' box. It was a great afternoon – Paul Tait played the sort of football that convinces me he is destined for the Premiership, Chris Whyte was outstanding and throughout the team there was hardly a poor display. We went down to the directors' room after the match exhilarated and optimistic – at last Barry and the team were producing the sort of results that made First Division football next season a distinct possibility. As we smiled and celebrated, Barry appeared on the television screen for a brief touchline interview with the Central Match crew. The interviewer drew particular attention to the performance of Jose Dominguez, our Portuguese winger:

'A great prospect for the future, eh Barry?'

'Yeah, he was wonderful,' said Barry, 'particularly as Barry Fry and Lil Fucillo nearly got the sack for buying him because David Sullivan thought he was absolutely useless. Anyway, got to go, right. See ya.' We all stood there astonished. All David could say was: 'That's a bit strong, isn't it?' I swiftly excused myself from the company and stormed straight down to the corridor where the dressing rooms are housed.

'Get Barry Fry out,' I said to an apprentice, 'tell him I want a word with him urgently.' I was steaming mad. David doesn't care what Barry says about him – he has always insisted on having his say as the man who owns the club. But, by the same token, he has chosen Barry to pick the team and if a player he doesn't rate is the man-of-the-match he is as delighted to be proved wrong as the manager is to be proved right. Standing in the kit room waiting for Barry to appear, I was beginning to feel really angry. Barry came through the door and, to my great surprise, he was almost nude. Barry stood there, in a tiny towel that just about protected his modesty, shivering and dripping wet fresh from the shower. He looked a very comical sight, but I was too angry for jokes at that time.

'What the fuck is going on?' I raged. 'Why was it necessary for you to say that?'

'Because it's true,' he replied.

'No, it's not,' I said. 'David might have thought he was limited at first, as did you but now he thinks he is the best thing since sliced bread. You know that, but you still have to have your little dig, your little comment. David doesn't care, because he owns the club, you don't get hurt because you've had your bit of fun. But how do you think Jose must feel now? He's played the game of his life and he's sitting in there thinking the owner feels he's absolutely useless. He's the only one that is hurt, he is the only one who has lost. No one wins by you saying this and it has got to stop. I am furious about this, I am furious with the pair of you.' All the way through, Barry is nodding and saying: 'Yeah, right, I can see your point.'

'And another thing,' I continued, 'if I say something to you about the football, or about a player, that is between the two of us and is part of our working relationship – I expect it to stay that way. If you confided in me about a member of your staff, you would not be pleased if my first move was to go to him and say: "Guess what Barry thinks of you?" That is not the way it should work, you should not keep telling the world our business. Anyone looking from outside Birmingham now would think you and David absolutely hate one another and it is a matter of time before you either get sacked or resign. And that's quite wrong, isn't it? Because he wants to keep you more than any other manager in the League, and if there is any manager who would get along with David, it's you. So I don't know why you don't get on with the job. If he wants to make comments that is up to him, you answer them on the pitch if necessary. At the end of the season you'll show who knows more about football. What is going on at the moment is totally uncalled for.

'It has got a bit out of hand,' said Barry.

It was only after I had stomped off back upstairs that I realized how people must have thought it strange that I should go into the players' areas like that. I would never have dragged Barry out of the shower myself, though – but I was so angry it never occurred to me there might be a degree of embarrassment. All I knew was I wanted to speak to Barry and I wanted to do so immediately. Now for David, and I returned to the boardroom for a less impassioned chat.

I told David about my conversation with Barry and gave him a similar view. 'Look', I said, 'I've had a word with Barry, and told him to stop sniping at you all the time. And if the press ring you, there is no law you have to answer their questions. If they ask about Barry, don't comment. The only reason he keeps responding is because he thinks you are chipping away at him. If you stop digging at one another this is going to be a happier place for everybody. Barry has got to learn to be more discreet.'

When Barry appeared in the boardroom it was as if he had finally started to see logic, although the atmosphere was awkward. 'You don't appreciate the problems this causes,' I said. 'It is not you getting five hundred letters saying everyone should support the Manager when, in reality, everyone supports the Manager and he has never been turned down for a single transfer, or a single request for anything. It is not you who has to front out the sponsors when they worry about bad publicity. It's me – and I've got the hump with it.'

Barry loves publicity. He loves the press, he knows a good story and he is good at telling them. And if he has a good tale, he simply has to tell it. Put those two combinations together and you can see why Birmingham has become a journalist's dream and this Managing Director's nightmare. Most clubs in our Division can't get in the newspapers; we can't get out of them.

Luckily, although Barry's televised attack on David was reported, the row between him and Mark Ward had not, so far, come to light. When we met the next day, we were able to hammer out the problems in private. Barry, Edwin, Mark, Lil and David Howell all came in and we sat around the table. Barry opened up the meeting in typical straight-talking fashion.

'It doesn't matter a fuck what Mark Ward wants to do,' he said. 'This is my team, my staff and we'll do it in my style. If I fuck up, a new manager can come in and do it his way, but until then I'm in charge and what I say goes.' Seeing as it was also the chance to coach that brought Mark to Birmingham – as our highest-paid player – Barry's words struck a chord with me. 'Basically it is my job on the line and, if I get the sack, I get it for doing things my way,' Barry concluded.

I had to agree. If Mark wanted to get more involved he had to start at the bottom, and watching the reserves was to be that start. It was not right for him to pass comment on a performance he had never seen and if Mark kept an eye on the reserves home and away he could take a greater interest at that level.

When we left I thought the air had been cleared. Barry had been allowed to get on with his job, while Edwin, too, had realized he was safe so long as Barry was in charge and we were not looking to replace him with Mark. As for Mark, he now had to prove himself as a coach and show he was willing to work and devote extra time to his duties. It was probably then that I started to warm to Barry. We had almost twelve months of problems between us, but he acted very intelligently over this issue and his arguments made sense. But his treatment of Gary Cooper was an important proving ground in our relationship.

It was 18 October, and two and a half hours before we were due to play Walsall in an Autoglass Windshields Cup game, when Barry came into my office.

'Bloody Gary Cooper hasn't turned up again.'

'What do you mean?'

'He hasn't been in for about five or six weeks because his kid's not well,' he said. 'Now he's rung in tonight to say she's been taken into hospital again and he can't come to the game. I don't know who I'm going to play instead because we've got so many injuries.'

I was surprised because only the week before Gary had told me his baby daughter had been given the all-clear and this seemed to me one sick-day too many. Barry had told me before about Gary's absences – a virus one week, a British Rail suicide the next, and plenty more time off for his sickly daughter. I decided to ring him and, to no surprise, Gary himself answered. 'It's Karren Brady, Gary,' I announced, 'I thought you were in hospital with your daughter?'

'Oh, er, I was just on my way back there,' he said, hesitantly.

'Well could you kindly tell me the name of the hospital, the name of the ward and the name of your daughter,' I said, 'because this has been going on for too long.' The phone went down with a click by way of reply, I knew I was on firm ground. The phone remained engaged for hours after but, by sheer luck, my dad Terry's printing business was in the same street in north London as Gary's house. I faxed a letter down for him to deliver, detailing the serious nature of our complaint against him and summoning him to a meeting at St Andrews the next day. Barry was even more upset than me, feeling rightly that he had been misled. When we got Gary's file out all we saw was a long list of club fines for absenteeism – and it appeared that if we wanted to fire him tomorrow we would have right on our side.

The chance to see Gary, let alone sack him, would have been welcome. At eight o'clock the next morning my phone rang at home and Gary announced he could not make our meeting as his girlfriend had to go to work and he had to stay at home to babysit. At that time in the morning I was not at my best and immediately lost it. 'You had this letter yesterday, in plenty of time to find a babysitter. You are a professional footballer and well rewarded for playing for us, not sitting at home minding babies. I want you in the office as soon as you can.' And this time it was my turn to abruptly hang up.

Gary arrived at St Andrews at 11.30 a.m., but not with the explanation we had been waiting to hear. 'I've been lying about my kid,' he admitted, 'she was ill, but she's over the worst now and is out

1 March 1993. I was touring the football
clubs up for sale with David Sullivan. The
Manchester Evening News called me a bimbo
but I knew exactly what the score was.

2 March 14, 1995: Barry Fry with Paul Williams and Steve Claridge. We were in the thick of our disagreements, but at least we had started to win.

3 Mark Bowler and Allan Robson – the commercial team! When I first arrived I had to sack most of the staff. Now we know the clowns by their dress.

4 David Gold, one of David Sullivan's partners at Birmingham City (with me and Paul Peschisolido). When we first took over Birmingham City there was a lot of hostility from the local papers – so-called cockneys taking over a brummy club! But that turned out to be the least of our problems!

5 Doug Ellis one of the Midlands' legendary football Chairmen. I knew I had started to do things right when this great man accepted me.

6 St Andrews under construction summer 1994. When we first arrived the place was falling to pieces. I'd seen better facilities in a Bangkok lavatory. The stadium now holds nearly 30,000 seated.

7 There was some enjoyment amongst the grief during those first few months. We did try and foster a family atmosphere in the club. This was the first family fun night where I took on the face painting.

8 November 1994: our hopes catch fire instead of going up in smoke. Playing Shrewsbury Town we won 2–0. Things were going right for Barry. If they hadn't he would have been out by Christmas.

9 The Management (from the left: David Gold, Ralph Gold, me and David Sullivan). A determined team. We aim to win the Premier League. Nothing else will do.

10 Gary Cooper: one of our best players.
Barry told me he should be given a second
chance. I didn't want to. Barry was right. It
was a turning point in our relationship.

of hospital. It's just that I don't like the travelling and my girlfriend wants me in London. I don't know if I can come to any more games. I'll just have to keep you informed as and when the games come.'

'Gary, you've got two choices,' I told him. 'You can carry on earning a lot of money, I'll go down and have a word with your girlfriend and we can try to get something sorted out. Or you can be sacked and go on the dole for £40 a week. It's up to you.'

He looked me straight in the face, 'I'll think about it,' he said.

'Look, this is a joke, give me one good reason why we should give you another chance, because I can't think of any? You've lied to me, you've lied to the Manager, you've made us all look bloody stupid. There are kids out there who would give their right arms to be professional footballers and we are saying if you show you are committed to Birmingham City we'll do all we can to help you. Problems we can deal with, lies we will not tolerate. You've got to think seriously about your future, because a stable job has got to be better than just walking away and living on nothing.'

'I'll think about it,' he echoed, and the meeting ended.

A week later, Barry told me Gary had not travelled with the team or played in our match at Brentford on Saturday as requested – luckily for him we won 2-1 – but, for me, that was the final straw.

'He is taking the piss out of us all,' I told Barry. 'Contact the Professional Footballers' Association and tell Brendon Batson we are terminating his contract. He's been fined so many times he probably owes us money.'

We sorted out all the papers to end our association and Brendon came down to sit in on the final negotiations. What annoyed me most about Gary's behaviour was that we could not have tried harder to be fair and understanding. We hadn't fined him for not travelling to the Brentford game in case he had money worries and both myself and Barry had made ourselves available to help out with any problems. But it seemed no use – all our attempts to prevent this day happening had been rejected. Reluctantly, I told Barry:

'The decision is yours, but I don't think we have any option but to get rid of him. His career has hung by a thread for so long and if he won't abide by your decisions, then he has to go. If he stays he undermines your authority. He doesn't take his career seriously and nothing we tell him seems to sink in. He has even asked to be released and handle his own registration and I think we should no longer stand in his way.' Barry agreed. As far as I was concerned, the matter was over.

So it came as a bit of a surprise on 29 November, when Gary's name turned up on the team-sheet for an Autoglass Cup match against Gillingham. 'One more chance, Karren', said Barry, 'I'll give him one more chance.'

All I can say is thank God Barry did. Gary has been steadily improving these last few weeks, and last night he got into the team and scored. I'm not saying I understand Barry's methods, but after his patient handling of this affair I am at last beginning to appreciate them.

There have been times during our first twelve months together when I thought we would never click – never. I could not comprehend his style, he could not get to grips with mine. We are both from such different backgrounds I think we were on a war footing from day one and his handling of Gary Cooper proves our different outlooks. If I had been solely in charge, Gary would have been history. I don't think I was ever hard on him, but at the end when even the PFA seemed to be failing, that would have been his lot. Barry thought he could get something out of him, he listened to me, ignored everything I had said and followed his own hunch. And he was right. Barry Fry was right. He was right and I was wrong.

Chapter **5**

peace on

By expecting Barry to conform
to my ideas I nearly lost the
best manager Birmingham
could possibly have

Barry Fry's management philosophy has always been the same. 'I do things my way,' he says. 'When it doesn't work sack me, when it does let me get on with the job.' Had he said that on the first day we might have got on better at the start. But who knows. Now, for the first time, we are beginning to understand one another. Until now, I have found Barry's approach very hard to deal with. I like structure, I like knowing what is going to happen, when it is going to happen and what the results are going to be. Which is why Barry's often chaotic approach to the job will never find common ground with mine. What I didn't realize until now is that by expecting Barry to conform to my ideas I nearly lost the best manager Birmingham could possibly have. I'm not saying he doesn't still drive me mad, I'm not saying there are not mornings when I would cheerfully strangle him. We're not going on holiday or setting up home together. But we're managing – and that's a lot more than I thought we could ever do a few months ago.

That Birmingham City are now second in the league and look capable of at least making the play offs, if not winning promotion outright, has of course helped. Barry has proved himself to be a capable manager. He got us into the top three by Christmas as asked and we now feel a lot more confident about the future. But the most important thing we now appear to share is mutual trust. I think Barry now has a far greater idea of the demands on me as Managing Director, while I certainly understand that with all the pressure put on him by the supporters, he doesn't need extra aggravation from me. Had I known more about what makes Barry tick I would never have made him prove himself in such a harsh way. When I look back to the start of the season and how I treated him it makes me cringe. Imagine sending a football manager a memo and expecting it to mean anything? Imagine thinking you could use the same management techniques on Barry Fry as you would the head of advertising at Sport newspapers.

Maybe the fact the team is doing well has made people happier to take responsibility. I'm sure Barry no longer feels he is walking on coals, fearing for his job, worried to do anything that might incur his employer's displeasure. I blame myself for this. It is only natural that there should be a breaking-in period – but it shouldn't last twelve months as ours did. I think my mistake was in wanting Barry to be like our previous manager, Terry Cooper, from the day he arrived. I now accept there is no way two personalities are going to be similar in a job that lends itself to a highly individual approach. Terry might have been my cup of tea as a person, but Barry captains a more successful ship. When I study Barry's methods of discipline, I shudder. It appears to me the players come and go when they want, do what they want, train when they want and are totally without order. But that is Barry's way, not my way, and while we are top of the table I am not about to complain.

Most clubs employ a coach, not a manager, even if that is not the official job title. To me, a manager manages, whereas I would say Barry coaches, motivates and manages the players, but does not really like the rest of the organization of running a club, whether that is contract negotiation, deciding on transfer fees, or any other part of the business side of football management. I wasn't involved with those things when Terry was in charge and I think my problems with Barry began there. I expected him to run the club as Terry did, very structured, everything arranged, leaving me to sort out the commercial and marketing administration. Terry would walk in, present a schedule for a pre-season tour of Italy, complete with fixtures, hotels, flight times and costings. He would tell me who was going, who was staying behind and what those left behind would be doing while the first-team were away. He'd give me the date they were due to arrive back and then their pre-season schedule at home. It was lovely for me, exactly the sort of structure I had been used to. Then Barry arrived and it was like the world had turned on its head. Some players trained at this time; some trained at that time; pre-season was arranged last-minute; a visit to the training ground became a chaotic experience. Terry had kits reproduced for each player with numbers that corresponded to their numbers in the team. To a logical mind like mine, that was perfect. But when I first visited Barry's training ground I was horrified. Some players wore red, some wore black, some wore blue, there was even one bloke training in an overcoat. I left with my head spinning, it looked so amateurish. But if I didn't like it there wasn't much I could do: 'Like it or lump it' was Barry's outlook. Unfortunately he only expressed those feelings behind my back and if we had had it out in his first weeks at the club, maybe the first year would not have been so painful. Instead, I thought I could change him and he thought he could keep me happy by agreeing with everything I said and then ignore it.

I would propose a measure to keep discipline, such as weighing the players every week. 'Yeah, Karren,' he would say, 'we'll definitely start that.' Then two weeks later I would hear the players had never been weighed and get the hump. I took Barry's constant mantra of yeah, yeah, yeah, as agreement. Actually, he was saying it to get me off his back, like accepting an invitation from a friend to a party on Saturday. 'Sure,' you say, for a quiet life, knowing you'll come up with an excuse to cry off nearer the time. We've all done it. Except Barry had turned it into an Oscar-winning art form. No doubt he left the office thinking weighing players was a waste of time with no benefit whatsoever. He just didn't know how to tell me that. Barry lets players come and go as they please providing they play for him and do the work well on Saturday. Had I known he couldn't be changed from the start I don't think we would have had so many problems. I thought structure would make Barry more efficient, I really thought sending out memos on certain topics would help us get along. I envisaged a situation where we could sit down and discuss reports on player fitness, work out certain regimes for individual players and everyone would be happy. What I didn't realize was that Barry invariably left my office thinking: 'What the fuck is she going on about?' Memos mean nothing to a football manager, yet had we not been successful this season I would no doubt be sitting here now saying the reason Barry failed was because he was unstructured – and it has taken a long time for me to realize my mistake. I haven't given up completely, of course, there are still certain things I believe can be improved. But I am learning about Barry and he is learning about me. And I do trust him now, even when he suggests something that is an anathema to me, like taking the players away for a weekend booze-up. The day he suggested that I nearly fainted.

'But Barry,' I protested, 'at least wait until there is a gap in the season.'

'No, it will be good for morale,' he insisted.

A few months ago I might have gone off the dial. This time, I decided that if Barry thinks it will do some good, he's probably right. We came back and lost, of course. But the next week we didn't. Now we are in the top two I don't think Barry is so reluctant to make waves and I am certainly more willing to let him have his head, knowing that his methods are paying off.

Now we are getting on, it is easy to see how much damage our disagreements have caused Birmingham City. Instead of bickering about problems, we now sort them out. When Steve Claridge, one of our best players, went through a run of poor form I said to Barry we should get him in for a chat. A few weeks ago he would have told me to get stuffed and complained to David that I was poking my nose in and undermining his authority. I would have thought he just wanted an easy life and the whole thing would have simmered on. This time, he agreed, which meant we could both talk to Steve and ask if there was anything troubling him away from football and, if so, did he want to talk about it. He said it was simply a poor run of form – I've got no solution to that, but at least he now knows he can come to us and we feel satisfied there is nothing untoward going on.

We did the same with a younger player nineteen years old and a good twenty pounds overweight. Our approach to him was slightly different.

'Look at you,' I said, 'at your age your fitness should put everyone at the club to shame. Instead you'll be finished here in a few months because you've got no future unless you start doing some work on your own. Barry says you are not putting in the effort and he and Edwin aren't going to stand over you while you do it. You need to be self-motivated. At the end of the season, if you're still fat and not playing, Barry won't get the sack, Edwin won't get the sack, Lil won't get the sack – you will. And there will be no point blaming any of us then, because it will be your fault and no one else's.' Now he has lost weight and is training really well, which just shows we can work together.

Had the situation continued getting worse and worse, one of us would have had to go. I thought he was digging at me all the time, in the papers, on television, exaggerating the trouble between us. When he announced he had been given three months' trial by Karren Brady I was furious. He knew about the Christmas review in August, why suddenly bring it up as if we had shifted the goalposts midway through the season?

'I'm not saying you don't have to watch your back,' I said, 'and I understand that if you got the sack you may not just walk straight into another job, so it would be a bigger problem for you than most. But no one is breathing down your neck, no one is about to sack you, no one is putting pressure on you. Blame me if it happens, by all means, but stop being so paranoid and covering your back because nothing has changed from the start of the season.' Bickering like that almost cost Birmingham promotion, but one signing – or the lack of one – proved the turning point.

I think the most constructive event in our relationship was our attempt to sign Kevin Francis from Stockport when David Sullivan was away on holiday in St Lucia.

When David left for St Lucia it was on the understanding that Francis was to become a Birmingham player. The day David flew out, Barry phoned to say the deal had changed and Stockport wanted £800,000 plus instalments. I immediately put a stop on the transfer until I had spoken to David. What is the most you will pay for Francis, I asked. '£600,000,' he said, so that was the bid we put in to Stockport. What I didn't realize was Francis had already been told the fee had been agreed and was on his way down to St Andrews to sign.

In the meantime, Stockport were not budging from £800,000 as the asking price and were now accusing us of welshing on the deal and upsetting their player. Upset was putting it mildly. When Francis heard he was returning to Edgeley Park he was devastated. Which left myself and Barry sitting in the office discussing how to resolve the situation.

'David told me we could go to £800,000,' said Barry.

'He told me £600,000,' I insisted, 'and I can't change that without his authority.' So we rang David.

'OK, go to £800,000,' he said.

Back we went to Stockport. Now the extras were the sticking point, money down after certain games, money after international appearances and other bits and pieces. So no deal. Finally, we settled on £400,000 down and four instalments of £100,000 over a period of time. And then Francis failed his medical because of a dodgy knee. So now we were left trying to rework the deal based on the risk he could suffer a career-threatening injury. We settled on £200,000 down and then three instalments of the same after certain games had been played. But David said no. Then he phoned Stockport direct. Now Stockport said no. But all the time Barry and I were coming closer together because we were getting a greater understanding of each other as people and professionals. It helped to realize the real power behind Birmingham City is not Barry Fry or Karren Brady, it is David Sullivan. Even going second in the League didn't do us as much good as our trials in signing Kevin Francis.

To finally reach an amicable working arrangement with Barry was a huge weight off my mind. David, the Golds and I wanted someone who had achieved success at our level, achieved success on a tight budget and could project the right image for the club. We had lots of other names to consider, but one by one they all fell by the wayside. Our biggest mistake was advertising the job, thinking it would give managers already under contract the chance to apply in private. All we got was a thousand applications from Midland Sunday

League managers claiming they could do it brilliantly if given half a chance. It appears that, in football, people like to be approached rather than put themselves forward. So we had to go out and find our next boss – but even that proved difficult. Ralph and David Gold had strong opinions and names were being put forward on a daily basis. Mike Walker was another suggestion, but Norwich were in Europe and we felt there was no way we could entice him to join a club at the bottom of Division One. The same was true of Trevor Francis, the supporters' favourite and a local hero. He topped a local newspaper poll as the choice of Birmingham City fans, but he was hardly likely to leave Sheffield Wednesday, a bulging bank balance and the Premiership to come with us. Another director put forward John King from Tranmere, and other advice was to take Martin O'Neill from Wycombe. There were so many names, so many differing opinions, it was hard to make a decision. But losing game after game, we could not afford a long delay. It was with that in mind that we finally decided to approach Charlton for Alan Curbishley, an ex-Birmingham player who had done a good job with Steve Gritt. But their Chairman said he was not available and not interested in joining us, anyway. So that was that.

By now, everyone we spoke to was putting forward a different suggestion, but the one name David and I kept coming back to over and over again was Barry's. He was a lively character, with a good record, who had brought success to clubs without having millions to spend. At that stage we didn't know how much money would be made available – certainly not as much as we have now spent – and his main appeal to me was his ability to operate well on a tight budget. He also seemed to have a lot of spirit and I had been impressed with the way he had kept Southend in Division One the previous season with only a handful of games to go. Bottom of the League, we were in even worse trouble and having a manager with the guts for the fight was vital to our survival. I didn't know Barry personally and had no knowledge of his character. His track record alone was good enough for me and David. He was our man. Now we had to take that view to the board. I thought there would be a greater chance of him going places with Birmingham than there was at Southend, and I didn't envisage many problems getting him to St Andrews. That was my first mistake. The board decided to go for him and by coincidence I met Southend's Chairman Vic Jobson in the directors' box at our game at Nottingham Forest the same week.

'I'm going to fax you a formal request to speak to your Manager,' I said. 'I thought I should let you know in advance.'

'Absolutely no chance,' he replied. 'Barry is not going to leave me and I am not going to let him talk to you. Find someone else.'

Realizing he was upset, I tried to placate him. 'Look,' I said, 'don't make a rash decision in the heat of this moment. Get the fax, have a think about it and maybe we can talk.'

'Forget it,' he insisted. 'You've got more chance of getting Alex Ferguson than you have Barry Fry.'

I left feeling glum, a mood not helped by another defeat, but on the way out I met Barry, who obviously hadn't shared his Chairman's views. 'I'm interested,' he told me, 'very, very interested.' So the next day I went ahead and put our request to approach him in writing. Behind the scenes, Barry has since told me, he was driving Vic mad to let us talk, even letting it be known through the press that Birmingham was interested in him. But all we received in reply was a fax from Southend saying we could speak to him, but we couldn't offer him the manager's job. It was a farce. What were we supposed to discuss? The weather? So I contacted Barry.

'We can speak,' I said, 'but I cannot offer you a job while you are still employed by Southend. But come to see me anyway.' I'll never forget the day he breezed into my office.

'Hello, gorgeous,' he said, 'how are you?' It was then I noticed he had another man with him.

'Who's that?' I asked.

'That's Edwin Stein, he's my assistant,' I was told.

'Oh hell, Barry,' I said, 'we haven't got permission to speak to him. We're going to get into trouble for this – couldn't he wait outside?' But Barry had this way of steam-rollering everyone into doing what he wanted and we did want him as our manager. So I showed Barry around St Andrews, while trying to ignore Edwin's presence as best I could. At the end I explained our predicament to Barry.

'If you cease to be employed by Southend there will be a vacancy for you at Birmingham,' I said. 'But obviously we cannot wait until the end of your contract.'

'That is OK, then,' he revealed, 'I've got a clause that I can buy-out my contract with a six-month payment.' This he duly went back to Southend and did. Then he phoned me. 'Right,' he said, 'I've bought out my contract, Edwin has bought out his. We're free.'

'As long as our lawyers put you in the clear contractually, this is all agreed,' I told him. 'Meet me at the Hyatt Hotel in Birmingham at nine o'clock tomorrow morning and we can run through the players, the training and put you in the picture about the whole club.' The next day I walked into a meeting with Barry, Edwin – and a third man. I experienced an incredible feeling of déjà vu.

'Who's this?' I asked.

'It's David Howell,' said Barry, 'he's my other assistant.' Suddenly, we had gone from employing a manager to taking on three people. I was understandably reluctant, but Barry was quite insistent. 'I can't come without David,' he said, 'he's my man on the training field, he looks after a lot of tactical things for me.'

'But we haven't got permission,' I explained. 'What is your con-tractual situation?'

'I've spoken to the Professional Footballers' Association because I am under contract as a player at Southend,' David said. 'Because I'm coming as a coach and because of my age I can terminate it at anytime.' So then we were three.

As far as I was concerned, the job was done. Except the next week things got complicated. First, Barry rang me to say he was leaving Southend. Then Vic called to say he had signed a five-year contract. Then he was arriving tomorrow. Then, they were supposedly all in the office at Roots Hall crying together and no one was leaving once more because Vic was ill and they reckoned the shock would kill him. And I was sitting in my office at St Andrews not knowing what the hell was going on and thinking that having gone all out for a manager we were now facing the humiliation of him turning round and snubbing us. I thought I had made a huge mistake and, according to Vic, so did Barry. Now I know him I realize it was another case of Barry agreeing to everything for a quiet life. He agreed to join Birmingham to keep me happy, then said yes to Southend's offer of a new contract so Vic would not be upset. In the end, I think what made his mind up was that Birmingham were a bigger club than Southend. The bigger stage suited his ambitions and, without the pull of our reputation, I'm not sure we would ever have got him. But, although the week-long delay didn't benefit Southend in keeping him, it made a huge difference to them financially, once they reported us to the Football League for illegally poaching their manager. Barry's dilemma was far from a private matter and all week the story had been back-page news. David Sullivan's comments to reporters that he always got his man and Barry Fry was the man for Birmingham, that he knew he had the job, that he only had to pay off his contract to leave Southend and that he would be our manager in two days, all helped seal our fate at the Commission. The whole thing should have been kept quiet and then Barry could have resigned as a free agent and quietly arrived at Birmingham, the way

Brian Little left Leicester only to pitch up at Aston Villa a few days later. Southend's argument was that Barry would not have resigned unless he knew he was going to a job at Birmingham, and they were right. Unfortunately, the world and his wife knew he was coming to Birmingham, too. It is ridiculous to suggest anyone jacks in their job without knowing their next move unless the situation is very extreme – and Barry's wasn't. I'm sure he would still be at Southend now were it not for our interest. But it could be argued that Brian Little's departure was in many ways identical and Villa only escaped punishment by handling the whole affair with more skill and tact.

At the time I thought it was a complete sham – and much of what went on within the four walls was farcical – but, looking back, had the situations been reversed we would have been livid. Southend didn't just lose their manager, they lost most of their management team, and the size of our fine would not even buy a halfway able defender these days. Barry has got us to the top of the table, halfway to Wembley and tying with the likes of Liverpool. Southend have done little since his departure. While it is impractical not to expect a club to 'entice' a manager to take their job, I can understand why Vic Jobson felt so aggrieved.

When we turned up for the Commission, David, myself and Birmingham's solicitor Henri Brandman were in one corner, Vic Jobson and Southend's QC in the other and in the middle sat three Football League men, chaired by Gordon McKeag. I thought the whole affair would be conducted in a sensible, orderly manner, much like a court case – instead, the gloves came off, and it developed into a verbal brawl. The QC whipped out a selection of what seemed like 1,500 interviews with David and quoted from them at random, Barry complained about the money Southend owed him and claimed he would have left anyway, while waving a never-ending collection of payslips as evidence. Before we went in we had discussed how we would let Henry, our solicitor, do the talking and behave in a way that was right and proper for the football club. But once the meeting commenced, it was a complete free-for-all. In the hullaballoo, certain points got lost completely. No one ever mentioned that Barry had bought his contract out, they were too busy arguing nonsensically about payslips. Vic Jobson produced a Christmas card from Barry as evidence, and started quoting the message, which he claimed had significance. Then the QC brought out Barry's mobile phone bill with a flourish saying it proved that Barry was in regular contact with David Sullivan all through the vital week. If the scene had been on *LA Law* I would have laughed out loud. David Howell was called in and announced that the PFA had told him he was allowed freedom of contract. What a lot of cobblers that turned out to be. The Secretary from Southend was produced to claim the original fax had not been received, then Barry started telling Vic he loved him and got out his own Christmas card. The reason he gave for quitting Southend was so obscure I don't think he even understood it. By this time I was ready to dismiss the entire Birmingham side of the room and fight them all on my own – it would have been easier. Then their QC decided to play his Perry Mason card.

'When did you resign from Southend?' he asked Barry. He was told the date. 'And when did Edwin resign?' Barry replied. 'So you quit two days apart?'

'Right.'

'Then how come your letters of resignation,' he said, his voice rising sharply for dramatic effect, 'are written in the same typeface?' What bloody difference does that make, I cried. It was left to Edwin, though, to present the most eloquent case for the prosecution – inadvertently, of course. Before the case we went through the evidence with him. I wanted to follow Barry, I paid up my contract and left, that was the story. Unfortunately, it proved a bit tough to remember.

'What did you think when you heard Barry was going to Birmingham?' he was asked.

'Well, I said to him in the car up at Birmingham, you've got to take that job,' he replied, as we cringed and I begged someone to shut him up.

'So you were with him when he was offered the job?'

'Yeah, they did talk about one when we were up there. I said you've got to take it Barry, for your career because, I mean, none of us was happy, I mean, look at my payslips. . .'

That was it – game, set and match to Southend. By now it was nearing midnight and we knew we had no hope of winning. The Commission's verdict was guilty, guilty, guilty – punishment to be decided.

Southend were pushing for a twelve-point deduction, but a day later the Commission gave us a £130,000 fine. We were gutted because it was double what others had paid – although the fact we took a management team rather than merely a manager obviously influenced their decision. Had Barry's appointment not worked out I would have been spitting feathers about the fine, now I look back and see it as money well spent.

Of course, now things are going well, David and the Golds feel the same. The better results become, the more the farce of the Commission becomes a dim and distant memory. As for Barry, I think he has changed in many ways and is actually at last realizing we are all behind him. I don't think there are many better boards to work for, and few others who would take the stick we do from him and keep backing him up with money. If Barry came to us for a loan he would get it, not as one last act of good faith, as a gesture of our continued support. He is still our man, every week, every month, providing he does the job well. At last we are getting somewhere. Fingers crossed.

Chapter **6**

priorities

I walked him down to the
operating theatre. I made so
many deals with God for him
to be OK that I should be ten
foot under myself

When David Sullivan told me that he had to have a heart bypass it was the worst day of my life. In all the years I have known David he has never been ill, except for the odd cold. He does not drink or smoke. It was a hard blow. The trouble started when we were watching our game against West Bromwich Albion on Tuesday 27 April 1994. We were desperate for a win. Nearing the bottom of the table, but still hoping to stay in Division One, we only had three games left and were 1–0 down. Then a great goal by Steve Claridge took us level, Louie Donawa scored the goal of the season, and David was, as usual, on his feet applauding the team. He sat down and I noticed he was looking a bit grey.

'What's wrong, Dave?' I said. 'You don't look well.'

He looked anxious and said, 'I've got a pain in my chest.'

'Look, Dave, you must go to the doctor and have it checked out to put your mind at rest.'

He felt that it was probably nothing but went the following week to have a stress test. The results were not good and he had to have an angiogram. He took his mobile phone with him as the angiogram test takes a few hours and he was not allowed to move while the test was being done. We spoke on the phone for over an hour as we waited for the results. It turned out that things were not just bad, they were desperate. The three main arteries in his heart were blocked, one by 82%, the second by 91% and the third by 80%. He needed a triple heart bypass. I was devastated. The main concern was that he would have to slow down and take it easy, but he is so energetic that I wondered whether he would really be able to.

When it came to the operation he was understandably very nervous, but most of all he was angry. I went to the library for the day and read everything I could about heart problems and bypasses, and I went down to London to spend the first few days with him when he had the operation. I was with him when he had his pre-med and walked him down to the operating theatre. I made so many deals with God for him to be OK that I should be ten foot under myself. The operation took hours, but finally the doctor came and told me that things had gone well and that he was in intensive care. I pulled myself together, expecting to see Dave with tubes and monitors all over him, hanging on for his life in intensive care. As I walked in I saw that he was sitting up having a cup of tea. I was astonished by the clarity of his eyes. He looked better than most people do when they have just had even a minor operation. He was in good spirits, but a little tired. He was even trying to read the paper, and complaining that the print was jumping around all over the place! We had a laugh looking at his scars – I was so happy that he was OK. His first question was about the team, so I knew he was going to be fine.

I brought in a diet specialist to see him at the hospital. David is a fussy eater – he has spent nearly all his life eating steak, chips and chocolate! All this had to stop.

'Muesli and bran for you,' said the dietician.

'I'd rather starve!' he replied.

After the op, Dave took it easy for about a week. He still works far too long hours and far too hard, but he is now two stone lighter, works out every day, looks fit and feels good. He watches everything he eats, and won't touch a chip, unless the Blues have won and we have chips in the boardroom after the game – then he allows himself one!

When I look back at all he went through, I realize that the problems at the football club are pretty minor in the scheme of things.

When I first tarted to work with Sport Newspapers I was employed by LBC as a sales person. Sport was one of my clients, and it was my job to get them to advertise on LBC and the Independent Radio Network. David was uninterested. 'No one listens,' he said and put the phone down. I had just started my new job and wanted to make a good impression. I had to get my first client quickly, so I rang him back.

'I need your help, I'm new and I have to make a good impression, surely you can see your way to spending a few grand.' I thought I would try the friendly approach.

'No,' he said.

'Please let me put a package to you to look at.'

'No, but if you come up with some sort of deal that I cannot refuse I'll look at it.'

'Let's look now,' I replied, and we eventually agreed that I would put *Sunday Sport* advertising on LBC for nothing but if there was a lift in sales in the London area he would pay for the advertising space – and if he didn't see a lift in sales . . . I put the phone down and thought, 'holy shit, I've only been here two minutes and I'm already giving the space away!' I told no one of the deal and made the advert, which went out that weekend.

On Monday morning when I got in to work David had already phoned. 'I'll take it all over the network.'

It was the best deal I had ever done. Dave would go from spending nothing on Independent Radio one year to spending over £2,000,000 the next.

David Sullivan was my first client and remained my only client. I made all his adverts, booked all his space and in my spare time ran his press and promotions. It was an obvious move to work for him full-time. Only six months after starting my new job at LBC, I was off to Eagle Wharf Road on £28,000 a year as Sales and Marketing Manager of *Sunday Sport*. I was nineteen years old.

In my working life I had worked for just two companies, Saatchi and Saatchi and LBC. Both had smart offices, in the smart part of London. I drove to Eagle Wharf Road and thought twice about even getting out of the car! There was this run-down warehouse in the middle of an industrial estate and this fire door with a sign that said 'SUNDAY SPORT' and a picture of a girl with the biggest tits I had ever seen. Apparently this was 'Tina Small', whose chest was 55EE! I walked into an office. It should have been condemned years ago. The place was open plan, and the typewriters were ten years old – the kind you have to bang away at with half the letters missing. People were spread all over the place and the whole staff amounted to fifteen or twenty people. I walked in and said, 'I'm Karren Brady, the new Sales and Marketing person.'

'Oh well, you can start by making the tea.' I made five hundred cups of tea that day.

It settled down and I found my feet. Soon after tea-day I phoned David and told him that I was appointing him a new advertising agency and part of the deal was that I would have an office in their building. I told him the only thing I was going to get done working at Eagle Wharf Road was to cut down the tea lady bill.

I took up my new offices at Squires Robertson Gill, our new advertising agency, and I never looked back. We did not have a sales team. All the space was contracted out to a third party who sold it on our behalf. Within a few weeks we had our own team, based in two offices in London and Leicester. We sold classified and display ourselves, and suddenly we were making more money than ever before.

When we started to branch out and become a full daily national newspaper, the *Sport* was a small ship, tightly run and making enough money for us to try something new. We started by launching *News & Echo*, a 'straight' newspaper – no sex, no phone lines, just plenty of news and sport from East Anglia and the North East. Unfortunately, the newspaper never really got off the ground, and after a few months it folded. But as always David was still keen to take on new challenges, and it was then that the football fun started.

David and I often talk on into the night. If we had just cleared the corner. If the ref hadn't been blind and we had got that penalty. If the player had stuck his foot out – it could have been a different game. By the end of two seasons you realize that a win is a win and it doesn't matter how you get it just as long as you get it. However, you do want to win some games more than others, for reasons that are not always straightforward.

In February 1995 we loaned George Parris to Brighton. Liam Brady, their manager, is a hero of mine, so I was happy to help him out. He wanted to take George on loan but could not afford his wages. He phoned and asked me if I would be prepared to allow George to go on half wages. Basically, would I fund half the cost of him playing for them? Barry did not mind doing the deal, as he had said George was not in his plans and to get back some of the wages was better than having him loafing around. I spoke to David, who was not that happy.

He believed that George was great back-up and, should we get any injuries, he would get his place back. Barry was not convinced and therefore I agreed with Barry that George could go on loan, but on full wages for the first month, and if he stayed for an additional two months we would allow them to pay just half his wages. The Chairman of Brighton phoned to thank me, and George was on his way. George was happy there and the extension beyond a month was agreed. Some months later, in April, David phoned to point out that we were playing Brighton in two weeks' time. By then we needed just two wins to clinch the League Division Two Championship and he did not want his own player playing against us at home on this very important match. After all, can you imagine the embarrassment if George scored the winning goal for Brighton and we lost our place as champions!

I thought it wouldn't be a problem. Liam was grateful enough to us when we loaned George to him, now he was only paying half wages, and it is pretty much an unwritten rule in football that loaned players do not play against their home club. Barry was convinced that when he let George go on loan to Brighton he had agreed with Liam that in the event of the player being there for three months Liam would not play him against us. Therefore no problem, or so I thought. We faxed Brighton a letter asking for their confirmation that George Parris would not be playing on Saturday 29 April, but got no reply. Brighton, it appeared, were more interested in how many tickets they were getting for their supporters for the away end. We had suggested 200, based on their average away attendance, and upped it to 500 after speaking to the League. Brighton were obviously not happy, but we were expecting a sell-out crowd and, knowing their average level of support, we did not want to give them the whole away end of 4,000 seats thereby leaving thousands of empty seats that we could have sold to Blues supporters.

It was now that I decided to phone Liam myself about George.

'Hi, Liam. I understand that we have still not had your reply confirming that George Parris will not be playing against us on Saturday.'

Liam was not happy. 'What do you mean by coming on the phone and telling me who I should or should not play?'

'Come on, Liam, my board would be terribly disappointed if you played George, especially when I talked them into lending him to you on half wages.'

His reply was blunt: 'I did *you* a favour by taking him and I'm not grateful at all. Last time I came to Birmingham I was shoved in the back of the stand – that's not how I expect to be treated.'

Thinking I had completely lost touch with the conversation, I asked him what he was talking about.

'When I came to watch a match I had to sit in the stand.'

Look, Liam, if this is all about where you sat in the stand then I am sorry, but I know nothing about it. If I knew you were coming there is absolutely no way that I would put you in any seat other than the directors' box.'

'You should know the treatment I got because it reflects badly on your club.'

'I know, and I am sorry, and it will never happen again. Now what about George Parris?' I said.

'I had not decided what to do, but now you've come demanding that I don't play him I might just play him.'

'I am not demanding, I am just saying that we did you a favour by lending him to you at half wages, and my manager tells me you agreed not to play him when you took him on loan,' I said.

'What a load of rubbish. I did you a favour by taking him on.' Then SLAM – the phone went dead. That's the last time Brighton get a favour from me.

Saturday approached and I wondered what Liam was going to do. I had already written to the Chairman saying how upset I felt. The

Chairman was very helpful and said that George was going to play sub. This was a good compromise.

Not long into the game we are two nil up and I am jumping up and down like a lunatic, much to the dismay of the rest of my directors. Sudddenly it starts to go wrong. Cooper gets sent off and Brighton score a goal. It's 2–1. Straight after half time they get two more – it's 3–2 to them. God (or the ref as he was often called) was looking after us though, one minute to go and we got a penalty. It's a draw. They still think it wasn't a penalty. I think it was, *and* I think that we deserved to win as we played some great football, but a draw is a draw and we march forward with two games left. In the end George didn't play, but I have never spoken to Liam since that day.

We went on to play Bradford at home. The League had brought the Division Champions Cup with them: all we had to do was win and we would be crowned Second Division champions at home and finally, after a long season, we would be back into the First Division. The atmosphere in the ground was electric. We were expecting to win. Bradford had nothing to play for since they were half-way up the table, with no chance of being in the play-offs and in no danger of rele-gation. We were looking forward to the game, thinking of the cup and of next season back in the First Division.

Bradford started at 500 miles an hour. I felt like checking the tables again. Maybe they were going for promotion rather than us. I have never seen a team fight so hard. We could not have scored if we had an open net – which we did have at one point – it was one of those days! The Directors of Bradford were jumping up and down and laughing every time we missed a chance. You can imagine what we all thought of that.

'What are they so bloody pleased about?' I said. 'After all, we have got a lot to lose if we don't win today.'

In the end we drew 0–0 and the Division Champions Cup was put back in the box.

I didn't bother going to the boardroom for fear that I might say something I would regret. All the Bradford Directors were leaving, congratulating themselves and smiling as if they had won the FA Cup. I went in later, and Barry, David Gold and Ralph and I sat talking about the missed chances until the small hours of the morning. I later found out from Bradford's manager Lenny Lawrence that the reason the team and Directors were so fired up was that the tannoy announcer said before the game: 'After we win today we will be having a celebration and looking forward to Division One. The players are now going to do their lap of honour!' No wonder they felt cheesed off and pleased that we did not beat them. Sorry to everyone at Bradford for thinking the worst!

Chapter **7**

baby Brady

I learned a lot about the male ego, how easy it is to manipulate men, once you know the secret

11 March, 1995: Leyton Orient. We won
3–2. We were now on top and racing towards
the Second Division title. For once we
couldn't do anything wrong.

12 At last we were commanding the Second Division and the players could relax and pray for a win. At the start of the season the praying was for real.

13 Paul Peschisolido. The rumours started to fly that I was involved with one of my players. The tabloids thought this great sport. Paul got on with the job – here against Derby. I for once said nothing.

14 David Sullivan at the AWS final. It was a
dream come true. We won 1–0.

15 April 23, 1994: the AWS final. 78,000 fans,
more than attended the Coca Cola Cup. We
were on a roll.

16 Just engaged, June 11, 1994. By then the
club was winning, I had got my bloke and it
looked like we would be promoted.

17 My father Terry Brady. I was brought up
to believe I could do anything. Work like
mad and don't take crap from anyone.

18 A happy ending? June 10, 1995: Paul and
I on our wedding day. We had won the
league, Barry was our best man and I had
learnt a thing or two about life.

After all the aggro, on 22 April we were through to the final of the Auto Windscreen Shield and on our way to Wembley! What a great feeling! Unfortunately, that joyful feeling lasted about five minutes, until the tickets went on sale.

We really wanted to prove that we could make this competition big, and we decided to promote it as it had never been promoted before. We worked very hard on it, and we amazed the football world by breaking all the records for attendances. We had 'Kids £1 Adults £5' games. We promoted the game on radio, in the local newspapers and wrote to our 26,000 supporters. One of the promotions was that any person who had ticket stubs for the preliminary rounds would get a ticket for the final at Wembley. We had been sent 45,000 tickets for the final and we had to guarantee a maximum of 20,000 for the stub holders, leaving us with 25,000 for season ticket holders. We knew that some of these would also have stubs, so that there would be some over-lapping, but until we found out how many stub holders were going to take up their allocation we did not know how many tickets we could give each season ticket holder. Keeping enough tickets back for one each (these were the best tickets in the ground), we put them on sale to stub holders first. Season ticket holders were soon up in arms, because the press had reported that they would not be getting their tickets and that we had not looked after their interests. As usual this was complete bullshit. In the end we sold every ticket we had, and everyone who wanted to go got a ticket. The tickets had to go on sale at the weekend, otherwise there was no way we would be able to service normal league match tickets since we worked all weekend anyway – most of us for at least twelve hours a day – reconciling money, counting tickets, dealing with queries. It was terrifically hard work, but we were going to Wembley and everyone pulled together. After the weekend I didn't feel well. It was hardly surprising, considering the abuse I had taken from season ticket holders frightened that they would not get their tickets, whipped up into a frenzy by the media. Things gradually quietened down as tickets were sold, but I still did not feel at all well.

I felt sick at the slightest thought of anything, all the time, every hour of the day. I got home late on Sunday night and my best friend Charlotte phoned me to tell me she was pregnant. 'That's fantastic news! How do you feel?' 'Terrible, sick all the time at the slightest thought of anything, all day long.'

Sounded familiar.

Surely I could not be pregnant. I was getting married in less than six months and had too much to do. Wembley was only a few weeks away, and then there was the rest of the season to contend with. Being pregnant did not bear thinking about. I put it to the back of my mind.

The following Monday I had to travel to London for a meeting. I was waiting at the station and bought a pregnancy test. All along I was thinking, 'it's just the flu, I don't know why I'm bothering'. I did the test in the toilet on the train. On the packet it said, if you see two pale blue lines, blardy bla, you are pregnant. My two lines were navy blue. I couldn't believe it, I was laughing out loud, and people were banging on the door of the loo. I popped my head around the door and said to the ticket inspector, 'Do I look pregnant?' He said, 'How the hell should I know? Show me your ticket.' I skipped down to my seat and phoned Paul. He just kept saying, 'No, really? Wow.' We spoke about it and both agreed that it was unexpected but great news. We would keep it to ourselves for three months and then tell everyone. I phoned Charlotte and it turned out that our babies were due on the same day. We had always been close, but this was crazy. I had met Charlotte at school and we had always remained good friends.

I often say that I gave up my young life to get ahead in my professional career, but that is not entirely true. I had my young life between the ages of 13 and 17 when a lot of my friends were closeted in their rooms doing their homework. My parents put me in boarding school because they said it would calm me down. I had had a fight in my previous school and they did not want me to become a tearaway. Boarding school seemed boring, until Charlotte and I teamed up and became best friends. I'd tell my mum that I was round at Charlotte's house, and she would tell her mum she was staying at my place and the two of us would go to London until the early hours of the morning. It was 1982 and we used to go to places like the Beat Route in Greek Street. We would stay up all night and go home around 10 a.m. the next day and sleep it off. We were two bored, suburban teenagers and this was our bit of excitement. We'd talk our way into places. Then talk our way into getting drinks. It never occurred to us that we were running a risk of getting into trouble. We'd have a drink, have a dance, walk around the streets until we were tired, and then come home. We lived in our own little world. We didn't mix too much with the rest of the girls at convent school; they liked Duran Duran and we liked the Beat Route. We'd even fool the nuns into giving us permission to leave school at weekends. Charlotte would ring up from the phone box pretending to be Mrs Brady, saying she was picking me up at 1 p.m., then I would do the same, pretending to be Charlotte's mum. One o'clock would come and we would leave school laughing. We got away with murder – if our parents had known they would have wept! I learned early on how to look after myself, to fend for myself in different situations. It was good preparation for what I would later face.

At 16 I moved to Aldenham, a sixth form boarding school where boys outnumbered girls twelve to one. It was a totally different environment for a girl from convent school. It was sink or swim time, just as it was the day I walked into the exclusively male preserve of a football club. Had I not had this experience as a teenager I am not sure I would have been able to remain so strong later. You either had to get on with the guys or spend two years in hiding. I elected to get on with the guys and made some very good friends – friends I still see, friends I respect and friends I spent the best years of my life with.

During those two years I learned a lot about the male ego, how easy it is to manipulate men, once you know the secret. I can remember one afternoon at school when the lads had smuggled in two bottles of Malibu. The boys began pouring it into mugs and daring each other to down them in one. Malibu has got to be the sickliest drink ever invented, but I joined in. What I didn't know was that I was the only one drinking the Malibu – everyone else had water, disguised as Malibu. And so the mugs were being passed around and around and, never one to be outdone by a man, I was drinking more and more. After about eight or so, I began to feel terrible. I couldn't believe that everyone else seemed so sensible. 'She can't handle it, she's only a woman,' I heard someone say. I took the bait and continued drinking. Then at 9 p.m. the bell rang for study call, which is a register to ensure that everyone was back in house. How I made it back God knows! I was dragged, literally, across a field and propped up agaínt a wall while the names were read out. I managed a slurred 'yes' before collapsing in a heap on the floor. The following day the housemaster nabbed me. 'Brady, yesterday you were obviously intoxicated,' he rasped. I had to think fast.

'Don't be ridiculous, I don't even drink,' I snapped. 'I had a terrible period pain, time of the month and all that, and I didn't feel well!

'Oh, I'm so sorry, I didn't realize. Please accept my apologies.'

It was too easy, these men were just too easy.

Since then I have never looked back in my relationship with men. As a species they are entirely predictable. I left Aldenham thinking more like a man than a woman. I knew how to fight, I knew how to down a pint, I knew all the male jokes and male idiosyncracies, and I knew how to swear. I reckon those early experiences were what enabled me to feel comfortable later on at a football club, to exist in a world where a skirt puts you at an immediate disadvantage. No amount of male aggression or industrial language bothers me. I am not intimidated being the only woman in the group. Early on in football I didn't realize what a help this would prove to be.

I left school having had a pretty wild time but with the advantage that by the age of eighteen all my youthful energy was out of my system. Just when most people my age were getting ready to hit the town, I was ready to go to work – and that made a big difference to me. Everyone wanted to go to nightclubs; I was bored with them. Everyone wanted to go round the world; I had been doing my own thing since I was 13. Others wanted the freedom of a university education; I had spent my young life away from my parents, so that held no hidden mysteries for me. Besides, my school had its own social environment – even its own pub. What I needed in my life was the order a steady job would bring. I was ready to settle down and get serious, and anything other than going out into the real world would have dampened my edge. Companies came into my college the whole time looking for new blood and, as I had decided to work in advertising and marketing, the one that most interested me was Saatchi and Saatchi. When Saatchi's man brought in a load of chocolate biscuits from their United Biscuits account, that made my mind up – so just two days after I left school I joined Saatchis. It was 1987, the best time to work for them. They had just conducted another successful election campaign for Margaret Thatcher and the Conservatives. There was talk of buying out the merchant bank Hill Samuels, and they were bringing in major accounts one after the other. The standard company car was a Porsche and no one seemed to do any work beyond entertaining clients. That was Saatchi's whole philosophy – if the client has a good time, we'll keep the account, so entertain the hell out of them. They were probably quite right, actually, because no one seemed too keen to leave us. I can remember one boss at the company was quite a heavy drinker. His clients would come down from their Head Office and he would take them out for the weekend. Except this particular time, he had passed out on his sofa and as the office junior I was told to take them out instead, while someone sobered him up. 'There is a place on Goodge Street called Jacks,' I was told. 'Take the bigwigs there and hold the fort, and we will be along as soon as we can.'

'Come along, folks,' I said cheerily, 'I'll take you to a nice place and everyone will meet us there.' So off we trotted down Goodge Street until I found Jack's which, frankly, looked more like a drunken sailor's idea of a nice place. There was a tiny little door leading to some rickety stairs and into the dingiest little dive I have ever seen. It was a basement room with faded velvet curtains, and as I stood with our clients in the gloom I felt certain I was heading for disgrace and the sack. The place where we were meant to be was probably spelt Jacques and was a lovely French restaurant just down the road. I was buying them champagne in what appeared to be an illegal drinking den. There was horrible music playing in the background which suddenly rose to deafening proportions as the lights dimmed. Honestly, I thought, this place is falling to bits. Then from stage right a woman appeared and started stripping off. That's it, I thought, I'm history at the age of eighteen. My career is over in this seedy, grotty rat-hole. I stood rooted to the spot while this naked woman waddled towards the executives who were behaving like dogs on heat. They were grabbing her everywhere and cheering, and all I could think of is how I was going to explain this to my boss.

Then just as suddenly it was lights up, stripper off, and the first exec turns to me and says as if nothing has happened: 'So, Karren, how long have you been with Saatchi and Saatchi?' Hang on, I thought, maybe I'm not getting the sack just yet. Half an hour later everyone else from the office arrived and it was: 'Thanks very much, Karren, well done, see you on Monday.' Another lesson learned. I couldn't believe how these sober-suited gentlemen had turned into animals shouting 'Come here, doll' and grabbing the stripper's tits one moment, then back to their respectable selves as soon as the lights went up.

I was learning about business all the time. Other facets were equally eye-opening, if not as literally so. One of our clients was Boursin cheese and, as juniors, our job entailed going into supermarkets on a weekly basis to see where and how it was displayed. We had to find the manager and ask why Boursin wasn't in a prime selling site and whether it could be moved, then we had to go back to the office and file a report on the response and our progress. Then the next week we had to do the same. In all, eight weeks were set aside for Boursin to make steady progress from the bottom shelf to a prime selling site. It was, quite frankly, incomprehensible nonsense. But I discovered that if you rearrange a supermarket display, providing you also put the price labels in the right place, no one complains. What's more, it stays that way, because the shelf stackers just place the products above their labels. So in my first week I achieved eight weeks' work – but instead of praise, I got a carpeting. When I filed my report and told them the way forward was to go in there and do the job ourselves, I was taken off the project and accused of causing havoc. It was typical of a world I could never hope to understand. I wanted to get to the point, to cut to the chase. Hearing these people talk about progress reports was like hearing a TV interviewer pussy-foot around a subject when the whole nation is screaming: 'Ask the question!' There was a direct route, a quick and easy solution, but they couldn't see it and I soon realized if ever there was a group of people not quite in touch with the real world, it was the people in advertising. A friend of mine worked on a Persil advert which ran for thirty seconds – not a big production by any means. But it took five days to shoot. Wars have been won in less time. They even had a structure for promotion which meant you couldn't move up for three years, whether you were doing a good job or not. People were graded by how plush their office was. A novice would have a pot of coffee on the desk. A bit up the ladder you got coffee and a plant, then coffee, a plant and a second phone – you knew you were destined for big things if you had coffee, a plant, a second phone and newspapers. It was then I decided I couldn't wait for ever and con-tacted LBC.

I lost my baby on Thursday 4 May. The day that the news of my preg-nancy appeared in the *Sun*. Paul and I had waited three months and all seemed well. I went for a routine check-up at the hospital. Paul and I were in good spirits and looking forward to seeing the baby on the scan. When the scan was placed on my stomach I knew something was wrong. The look on the doctor's face told me there was a problem. 'The baby has not grown as much as I would have expected. There is no heartbeat.' I knew straight away that the baby had died, and had an excavation the same day. This is without doubt the lowest point I have ever reached in my life. My life seemed to be going to plan: a great career, a great husband to be, a great football team that has reached Wembley and looked set for the First Division. It had all gone wrong, everything seemed to end for me on 4 May.

I know that having a baby at that particular time in my life was not planned. But I soon got used to the idea. It took all of thirty seconds for me to realize that it was the best, most wonderful feeling in the world. It took all of one second on 4 May to realize what was the worst.

When I came home it was hard to deal with. The press kept knocking on the door and sitting outside my house waiting to speak to me or Paul. Paul and I cried a lot, and I do not think that I will ever get over what happened to both of us. In some ways I feel totally responsible. If I had not worked as hard, if I hadn't been as stressed over the selling of the Wembley tickets, if I hadn't jumped up and down like a lunatic when we played Brighton, and so on. No matter how many people say 'It's just one of those things, it wasn't meant to be', you never stop wondering, never stop questioning yourself.

I want to start a family with Paul, and I hope that it won't be long before we do. But I find myself wondering: what if I did lose my baby because of stress at work? Worse still, what if it happens again?

Chapter **8**

Wembley day

A day that should have been a
dream was turning out to be
a nightmare

We always knew that we were going to Wembley. From the very first day we dropped to the Second Division we all thought, well, at least we will be at Wembley in the Auto Windscreen Shield. Even on 31 January, when we went 1–0 down in the semi-final against Swansea, drew level, then went 2–1 down, I still knew that we were going to win. We equalized again, and in sudden death extra time, against the run of play, Paul Tait hit the winner and we were in the final against Carlisle.

We had got there through hard work and determination, a sell-out crowd with nearly 50,000 Blues fans, the largest number of supporters from one club for any final since the war – what a record that is! It was going to be a great day. Another good thing: there was going to be a winner, because it was going to decided, if necessary, by sudden death, not by penalties. Thank God for that – our record on penalties during the season had been poor to say the least.

But with the big day just twenty-four hours away, things couldn't have looked more gloomy. A day that should be a dream was turning out to be a nightmare. Barry, it appeared, had attacked David Sullivan in the *Daily Express*.

The headline said, 'COR BLIMEY! BASIL'S TOLD TO LOSE AT WEMBLEY', and the story went on to say that David Sullivan had instructed Barry to play the reserves at Wembley and threatened to sack Barry if he won at Wembley and lost the promotion play-offs. Here is a part of it:

'. . . . David phoned me the other day, I got vexed with him because he was so negative about it all. He was saying that if I won the Auto Windscreens and lost in the Second Division play-off final at Wembley, he would have to get rid of me because of fan pressure. I've gone, "Are you sure?" He honestly believes that if we won the Shield and lost the play-offs, the fans would hang me. It's because he doesn't appreciate what this is about on Sunday . . . I've told David he doesn't know what he's got here. He's only been in this three years and he's in the Royal Box. Others have been in this game thirty years and not had this . . .'

From the outside it can look as if a continual war is going on at Birmingham, with Sullivan, Fry and managing director Karren Brady, all strong personalities, chipping in with their five penny-worth and all saying different things.

Sullivan announced after the Auto semi-finals, 'There will be tickets for everyone for the final.' There wasn't and it was chaos. The 3,000 who went to watch Birmingham play at Peterborough returned to find the ticket windows closed, none left. Season-ticket holders found themselves at the back of the queue.

The article then went into old details about Paul and me and our relationship and the reason as to why Paul had to go. We all know the truth about this anyway, but comments like 'Just because David Sullivan is God and he's saved us, it doesn't mean he's always right. And if he's wrong, I'll say so,' are not what you want to read the day before one of the highlights in your club's history.

Even more annoying was the final paragraph: 'The only thing that worried Fry about Sullivan and Brady was whether they were for real. "I was at Southend, happy enough, and then Birmingham say they want to talk to me. But I wasn't sure about David and Karren. So I go there and interview them!"'

Next I picked up *Today* newspaper: 'WEMBLEY WON'T TAKE THE HEAT OFF FRY,' screamed the headline. It was basically the same story. Barry is going to Wembley 'under the threat of the sack . . . Fry admits: "The axe is still hovering over my head." . . . "David . . . wanted me to play the reserves at Wembley" . . . etc. etc.'

I rang David straight away. 'What's going on?' I asked. 'The papers are full of the sack thing again and bust-ups between you and Barry.'

David was very down-hearted. The newspaper story had left him in total shock and disbelief – his conversation with Barry and the report in the newspaper were totally different. He said that he had spoken to Barry on Friday night. He had rung him not to put pressure *on* Barry but to take it *off*. It turned out that David had phoned Barry to say don't worry about the result at Wembley, we are doing well in the League and it now looks as though we will win the League or at least get into the play-offs. Enjoy Wembley – win or lose – the result is not as important as getting there. Even if you played the reserves it wouldn't matter, the most important game for the supporters is against Brentford next Wednesday. David, being his usual honest self, had explained to Barry that he was pleased with the way the team were playing and although if Barry had not got into the play-offs it would have been very difficult to keep the supporters happy, now that was all out the window and the pressure was off.

'Well, he must be mad,' I said. 'That all seems clear to me. How come Barry thinks you are negative and want to lose at Wembley and are threatening him with the sack?'

'I don't bloody know, and this has got to be one of the worst days of my life.'

David has always been very positive about the football side of things. He has always backed Barry financially and in discussions he has had with other board members and supporters – and now David had been unfairly attacked. I wanted to take the situation up immediately with Barry, but first I phoned the Golds and David saying that lies like this in the press were damaging and had to be stopped. They, however, took the view that for now, on the eve of Wembley and with the Brentford game next week, we would just have to put up with it. One director said to me, 'While we are winning in the League, Barry can piss all over me, but once we know our fate the pissing will stop and he will have to learn that he cannot speak about the board and David like this any longer.' The consensus was that we could not rock the boat, as the club's results were more important than anything else, and we would therefore tolerate this carping until the last game of the season and then a meeting would be called to lay down the law.

I woke up at the crack of dawn, realizing that Wembley day was finally here. Being nervous meant I felt sick, being pregnant meant I *was* sick! I'd been dreaming of the result all night . . . 8–0 . . . 8–8 . . . I was in goal, I scored a goal, we won, we lost – I thought of it all.

The phone rang and I knew that I wasn't the only one up at the crack of dawn. David was also awake.

'Have you read the *News of the World*?'

Here we bloody go again, I thought. 'Why can't he just stop talking to the press?'

'I wish I knew, see you at Wembley.'

Well, well, well, here we go again. The press was not, as we might have hoped, hailing the club's achievement in reaching the final, or the record Blues attendance, or even recalling how we got to Wembley. Instead it was full of inaccurate comments about the board.

We'd taken a lot of unfair criticism from Barry, who we continued to back one hundred per cent. We were supposed to have told him that we would not be providing the players with club ties and that they should buy their own. The *News of the World* also claimed that David Sullivan was 'refusing to foot a £600 hotel bill for the Birmingham players'. It even had an anonymous quote: 'One player revealed, "The lads were disgusted – but not surprised. This seems to be par for the course. They even wanted us to pay for our Wembley ties."'

None of this could have been further from the truth. Firstly, we had a very, very important game against Brentford, a top of the table clash, on Wednesday 26 April, just three days after the final. We all believed that whoever won this game would go on to be champions of the Second Division. This meant that we had to be careful how we planned the players' schedule in the week leading up to this all-important game. I had agreed with Barry that the players would stay in London on Saturday night and travel straight to the game on Sunday. Directly after the game the players would be back on the coach and back to Birmingham – no party, no getting drunk – we would arrange a party for the end of the season, win or lose. All was fine, until I spoke to Mark Bowler in my commercial department. I asked him where the players would be staying Saturday night.

'They are going to the Swallow Hotel. Barry said he had agreed Friday, Saturday and Sunday nights with you.'

Before I spoke to Barry I phoned David to check that he had not agreed to this. It appeared that I wasn't the only one who knew nothing about a three-night stay. It was the Wednesday before the final and I asked Barry to come and see me. I brought up the topic of the Wembley overnight stay. I told Barry that I was unhappy that he had instructed the commercial department to book three nights in the hotel before he had agreed it with me. He said that he did not want three, but only two, and that there must have been some misunderstanding. We all agreed – Ralph and David Gold were there too – that Friday night was a waste of time, but Barry said that he would prefer to stay in London on the Sunday, so that he could keep an eye on the lads, as – whatever the result – they would want to celebrate after the game. I agreed that this seemed sensible and we decided that we would pay for Saturday and Sunday nights at the hotel. The subject did not arise again, and as far as I was concerned the matter was closed!

As for the ties, again the story was all wrong. I had been out shopping in Birmingham and popped into a menswear shop to pick up something for Paul. While I was there the manager mentioned to me that the players had been in and ordered twenty-four ties at £45 each for Wembley, making a grand total of £1,080. Being totally unaware of the situation, I had had a word with Barry, who had said that the ties were being organized by the commercial department. It then appeared that we were trying to do a deal whereby they would give the lads the ties in return for a mention in the match programme. However, the shop was not satisfied with this and wanted a £7,000 executive box for the season . . . some deal! I spoke to Barry again and said that we could not possibly do this and that under the circumstances I felt that the lads should wear club ties. He agreed that spending over a thousand pounds on ties was a waste of money and that they should wear club ties. He ordered twenty-four ties, the kit man picked them up on the Friday, and that seemed to be the end of the matter. Then it turned out that Barry had not ordered enough ties – in fact he needed twenty-six. So in the end, as we wanted everyone to wear the same ties, he bought them all ties from Marks & Spencer. Why the club owner should be called cheap, when he knew nothing whatever about the ties, is beyond me!

The press were in full cry, even trying to get Dave and me to comment as we arrived at Wembley. The occasion was going from bad to worse, and we were all getting worn out and disillusioned. I trudged over to Dave, who said, 'The past two days are the worst days of my life, I have never felt so down and depressed. I have put in a lot of money and taken a lot of grief and now this. I am very depressed about the whole thing.'

He wasn't the only one. We were all depressed, me, Dave and the Golds. All of us were upset, worn out and depressed, and this was at Wembley! We had a mini meeting on the balcony of Wembley. 'This has to stop,' I said. 'We need to have a meeting and speak to him.'

'To think I bought the club for a bit of fun!' sighed Dave. 'And I'm having the worst time in my life . . . and we are winning!' Life is too short to be this unhappy. Things had to be sorted out.

The best bit of the day was when Dave and I went out on to the pitch. Imagine walking on to the Wembley turf with your club, having sold nearly 50,000 tickets! I doubt I'll ever have a buzz like that again. I was bursting with pride at the supporters who had turned up in such force. I managed to avoid Barry except for a few words on the pitch. Better left until the big meeting, I thought. Dave and I went back to our seats in the royal box. The game itself was not the most spectacular I have ever seen, but it was gripping, and at the end of ninety minutes it was sudden death – the first team to score would be the winners. We were sitting on the edge of our seats, and then Paul Tait scored. Sudden death and sudden roar. The crowd jumped up, we jumped up – we were winners, the Blues supporters were winners, Barry was a winner, and for the first time in a while we were all united in the fact that we had won. Pleased was an understatement, I'll never forget the moment when our captain, Liam Daish, held up the shield, it was very dramatic and full of passion. We knew that our problems had not gone away, but they were certainly forgotten for a few hours. I popped in to see the players, staff and management at the Hilton Hotel and then went straight home. I was definitely not in the mood for long celebrations. The problem of Barry and the press needed a solution. Partying till 3 a.m. was not it.

Chapter **9**

the championship
and the showdown

A lot was at stake and tensions
were running high

Things seem to have gone from bad to worse. That morning I picked up the newspapers, looking forward to seeing glorious pictures of the team at Wembley, and was faced with a picture of Paul Tait, who scored the winning goal, wearing a 'SHIT ON THE VILLA' T-Shirt on his back and a smile on his face. What a stupid idiot! The hero of the day had insulted our neighbours and ruined our family club image. How can you try and build a family image when your Wembley hero does something like this? Paul would need to be fined and disciplined by us, and by the Football Association for bringing the game into disrepute. Football was experiencing a lot of problems – match rigging, bungs, violence – and now Paul had added verbal abuse! He was going to have to be seriously reprimanded and fined two weeks' wages.

Barry and Paul turned up for the meeting. Barry was understandably angry and Paul was embarrassed. Paul claimed that it was a joke, a very bad one, and agreed to apologize to the Villa supporters and management and to our own supporters for bringing the game into disrepute. I wrote a letter to Doug Ellis, offering our sincere apologies to him for any embarrassment caused. Paul would have to wait and see what action the Football Association would take against him. I hoped it would be a severe reprimand and a fine, and not a three-match ban as some of the newspapers were suggesting.

The next major step for the club was to beat Brentford on 26 April. I was sure that whoever won would end up as Second Division champions. A lot was at stake, and tensions were running high. The game was a sell-out and the need for a win had never been greater. Brentford were as tense as us and there was little polite chit-chat in the boardroom. The atmosphere was electric, Francis and Daish scored fantastic goals and we won 2–0. God those players earned their money that night! We remained at the top of the table with only Brighton, Bradford and Huddersfield to beat!

The championship was finally decided at Huddersfield on a cold Saturday, with the Blues winning 2–1 and clinching our place in the First Division. We were obviously delighted and couldn't wait for next season. However, we were aware that the pending problem of Barry and his relationship with the board and the press still had to be dealt with. If we didn't approach the situation soon it was only going to continue, and we all felt that we couldn't work under that pressure.

Barry came to see me with David Howell (first team coach) about my refusal to pay hotel bills that David had been accumulating over the past six months. 'You've said that you won't pay these,' said Barry, flinging a handful of bills on to my desk.

'That's right, the situation is quite clear. When David and Ed joined us I told them that we would pay hotel bills for three months, we extended this by another three or four weeks, and I sent both of them a memo telling them that we would no longer foot their accommodation expenses. After all, five months into the job I would expect then to be making arrangements for themselves.'

'But Howell got injured. He couldn't drive and had to stay in a hotel nearby.'

'That's not part of the agreement. At no point did you or David come and see me with regard to extending the hotel accommodation due to the fact that David was injured. Barry, you cannot make up the rules as you go along. David, I am the Managing Director and I decide what bills we will or will not pay. You had a memo from me making your situation clear, if you wanted to make any changes to this you should have seen me. I make these decisions, not the Manager. As for you, Barry, you cannot give authority for anything unless you have clearance from me. I am still angry that you decided to take the player away to a health club, running up thousands of pounds' worth of bills.'

The relationship between Barry and me was strained enough as it was, but I felt I had made myself quite clear about the boundaries Barry was not to cross. David Howell of course was the loser, as he had got permission from his Manager and now was lumbered with hotel bills for six months. I agreed that David would not be punished for this and agreed to foot the bills, but told them both that there would be no repeat of this, and no more trips to health farms without prior permission. David Howell then expressed the wish for a contract to secure his position at the club in order that he could rent a house in Birmingham and would not have to foot any bills in the future. I agreed that he could have the same contract as both Barry and Edwin had – different money, but the same terms. Each party could dissolve the contract with six months' money paid, i.e. if Barry or Edwin wanted to leave or we wanted to sack them, six months' money was the compensation. This was agreed when Edwin and Barry came to the club and was similar to the contracts that they had at Southend.

Then Barry said, 'I thought that you would be offering us five-year contracts.'

'Why?' I said.

'Because we have won the Auto Windscreen and we have won the championship'.

I was quite taken aback by the request. 'Five years contract for taking us back to where we were before you joined us, and having spent millions of pounds on players! I can only think that you must be under the illusion that we are mad! If you had taken us up to the Division One play-offs or had continued to be in the top six of the First Division I could see such a request being realistic, but as all we've done is get back to where we were I really cannot. When you took over we had plenty of games to go, you spent plenty of money and we were sunk. Come back next season, if you do as well, then we will talk.'

Barry was flushed. 'That's not fair. I know loads of managers who have been in relegated sides and get five-year contracts.'

'Well they are not managers here, not of a big club like this. Do the business this year and we will do everything you want.'

I would like to think that Barry will be here in five years anyway, but managerial contracts are so often all one way. If the Manager is crap, you have to pay; if he wants to leave, he can and you get nothing. I was not moving on this.

Barry then exploded: 'You don't want me here, you've got Trevor Francis lined up, and you and David want me out.'

I said, 'Don't be ridiculous! Yes, we are having a few problems between us, you and the papers at the moment, but what benefit would there be in sacking you? You have had a successful season here, you have bought a whole team. Why would we sack you after doing so well? Barry, it just does not make sense. Think about it and you will see that you are being paranoid.'

With that Barry left. I was convinced that he believed that we genuinely wanted to sack him, though this would be sheer suicide. Also, if we had wanted to get rid of him we would have done it after all the slagging off we had received, we would not have held our tongue and kept our patience with him. We would not have been giving him money for transfers and trying to work things out. I picked up the phone to the owners. 'This situation has to be sorted out, it can go on no longer, let's have that board meeting and speak to Barry.' The meeting was scheduled for Wednesday 17 May, before our exhibition game against Notts Forest.

Before the meeting with Barry, there was a short discussion between me, David and the Golds. We wondered what we were going to achieve and how the meeting would eventually end up. Did Barry want to go – and was it that he had agreed to take up a position elsewhere – or was it about money?

We gathered around the table in the meeting room here in the office, all waiting to see how Barry was going to react and what he was going to say. I was determined to talk to him about this ludicrous situation with the press, and how so often things said in confidence were leaked, how our owner David Sullivan was undermined and how we looked to be at each other's throats. We also needed to discuss rumours that Barry was handing in his resignation to join Derby!

Barry bustled in with a 'Hi chaps' and seemed to be in amazingly good spirits. We decided to let him have the floor first, and it was agreed that Barry could put forward all his points and then we would answer them one by one.

Barry started by saying that he was unhappy that he had not been given a big bonus for getting the lads into the First Division and for winning the Auto Windscreen Shield. We explained that he got the same bonus as the players, which was substantial. Barry was not happy with that. He was convinced that we made millions from the Auto Windscreen and he felt he should get a big chunk of money. We said that we would think about it, and come back to him.

Then he talked about a current press report concerning how much money David was prepared to give Barry in the close season to buy players. It had been reported that this was going to be £3 million. Barry said that he believed the press report, and then was told by David that he had only £1 million to spend. It was pointed out to Barry that when we spent £800,000 on Ricky Otto it was on Barry's confirmation that he was buying a striker, but after two games it was clear that Ricky was a winger and not a striker, so then we still had to go into the transfer market to buy a striker. We had told him at the time that we could find another £800,000 for him to buy a striker (Kevin Francis), but Barry would have to understand that this was half of next season's income from ticket sales and that he would not be getting it twice. Barry agreed that this was correct. Nevertheless he had gone to the press saying that he had three pence to spend, that David wanted him to buy cheap and would not allow him to buy decent quality big name players, and that he would have to sell players to buy, and what kind of way this was to go forward . . . He had made no mention of the £1,600,000 he had already spent, or that he had agreed that half of this money was from next season as he had bought a winger, not a striker, when we needed a striker! David Gold pointed out that one should not believe everything one read in the papers and that in future Barry should contact David Sullivan direct if he felt that he needed clarification on anything in the press. David was adamant that he had not made any mention of £3 million to any journalists. David Gold also pointed out that board meetings should not be carried out via the press, discussion points should be kept between ourselves, and transfer fees etc should not be arranged via the press as this only served to warn other clubs of how much money we had to spend and therefore to jack the fees up.

Barry then went into the discussions that we had had regarding David Howell and hotel bills and said we had gone on to talk about contracts and that I had said that he would not be offered anything until he had proved himself further. I had made clear that football was more often than not short term, that the crunch season was next season and if he did well he would get the contract he wanted. He believed that he had earned the right to that contract now, and should not have to wait. He went on to say that I had offered the Manager's job to Trevor Francis over the phone last week.

'What a load of rubbish,' I said. 'I know my place here at Blues, and I know that it does not extend to offering the Manager's job to anyone. I seem to remember that you accused Jack of the same thing this time last year. I think that you have to stop being paranoid and get on with your job.'

Barry was suspicious because he had seen Trevor Francis in the boardroom when he had come to watch a game.

'Trevor Francis is a big star,' I replied, 'a hero at this ground. If he asks me for a ticket, what am I supposed to do – make him sit in the Paddock and go in the public bar? He got the treatment from me that is appropriate to his status, just as I am sure that you would be given a great welcome if you went back to Barnet to watch a game.'

'Yeah, you're right,' says Barry. 'But what about when David said I could talk to who I wanted when I mentioned that Derby were interested in me?'

David answered, 'I told you that I could not stop you from talking to anyone, which is quite true, but I did not encourage you – I just pointed out a fact.'

The game was about to start, and we called an end to the meeting. We told Barry that we would consider some of the points he had put forward, such as how much he earned for being promoted and how much he got for the Auto Windscreen, as well as a long-term contract, and we would get back to him as soon as possible.

'I knew this was about money,' said David, and the directors decided to sleep on it.

We spoke the following day and agreed a bonus figure for Barry. We also agreed that we would amend his contract and clearly lay out any individual bonus for him. So far he only had bonuses for promotion to the Premier League and for the Coca-Cola Cup and FA Cup. We amended the contract, added the Auto Windscreen and Anglo Italian Cup, and everyone was happy. For about a week!

Barry had taken a short break, and when he came back he had decided that the bonuses we had offered were not enough. The press speculation surrounding Derby continued, the reports from Derby indicating that his move to the Baseball Ground was imminent. Apparently he had spoken to Lionel Pickering and a deal had been struck. I asked Barry to come to the ground as quickly as possible so that we could sort this out once and for all. Barry was adamant that he had not spoken to Lionel and that this was just press speculation. With Barry sitting opposite me I telephoned Lionel at home.

'I am here with Barry and I want to know what's going on,' I said.

'Well is Barry there?'

'Yes, he bloody is. Now what's going on?'

'I spoke to Barry and we have discussed the position. I think you should speak to him,' said Lionel.

'But Barry, you *have* spoken to Lionel about the position, and from his tone he is expecting you to tell me some news, like you are leaving and joining him.'

'I am not leaving and I am not taking up the position at Derby,' he replied.

'There you are, Lionel, you have heard it for yourself.' Lionel sounded very confused. To me it was starting to feel like Southend all over again!

'Yes, I have spoken to him, but I want to stay at Blues,' said Barry.

'What exactly do you want, Barry? As soon as you tell me this I can sort something out and we can all be happy.'

Barry laid out his terms. The bonus he wanted was double what we had agreed with him, he wanted a three-year contract, still with a break clause and bonuses laid out for the future. I put Barry's demands to the board and they agreed them all. Barry was delighted and we announced it to the press. I cannot imagine what was going through Lionel's mind!

Barry agreed that from now on for all our sakes we would keep our business out of the press. We emphasized that next year would not be plain sailing and that if things got difficult it would be far better to be united as a club. That way the accusations in the press would stop and we would all live happily ever after!

So the outcome was clear: Barry would get what he wanted and we would keep our Manager!

Chapter **10**

looking to the future

That was definitely the worst time of my career, the most depressing few days of my life

Things are better now – still not plain sailing, but definitely better. Barry seems to have changed overnight, mainly because he has stopped criticizing the board through the press, and there is trust between us as there never has been before. It has been agreed that any comments made about the board will be honest and positive, rather than provocative and inaccurate. We will back Barry 100% both financially – he has bought eight players in the close season – and personally. We have told him that if the season goes wrong it is surely better for the board to be saying we are 100% behind the Manager, than to feel that it is pay-back time. Barry is relaxed and positive, and his attitude towards *us* is completely different from what it was a few months ago. Gone are the verbal attacks, the 'them and us' mentality and the cocky 'they need me more than I need them' attitude that we had to put up with around the

Wembley time. It is hard to believe that things have smoothed over so much since then. That was definitely the worst time of my career, the most depressing few days of my life, and I never want to repeat it, which is why it was important to get to the bottom of the problem with Barry so that we could find a path that we could both walk.

When I look back I realize that it all boils down to being appreciated. Barry felt that we never patted him on the back enough (with money as well as our hand, it turned out!), while we just thought that he was doing his job. Barry likes to be liked and likes to be rewarded – in fact more with words than money, I think. While we considered the success last season as 'doing the job', he would have liked us to think that he had saved the club single-handedly and should be rewarded with a Blues Knighthood – the handsome handshake! He got this, and got the respect of the supporters, but he would have won *our* respect sooner if he had spoken to us rather than given us the pressure he did via the media. We have had lots of ups and downs, but as we look forward to the 1995–96 season I feel more confident about our future than ever before.

Season ticket sales have almost doubled to 11,500, generating over £2 million – which is why we have been able to buy the players that Barry has wanted. We have certainly spent more than £2 million on nine new players, taking our tally up to forty-five. A lot of people have criticized us for having such a big squad, but I honestly believe that this will be what makes us this coming season. We are in four competitions, the FA Cup, the Coca-Cola Cup, the Anglo Italian Cup and the League, and what with injuries and suspensions you need good back-up. We have two first teams, all good quality players, all able to step into each other's shoes. Come Christmas, when other teams are flagging due to the small size of their squads and the injuries and suspensions, we will have players to spare. We have already sustained injuries to three of our top players: Kevin Francis, our £850,000 striker, Peter

Shearer, who scored valuable goals from midfield, and Dave Barnett, our centre-half, are all out until November or December, which is why we have bought replacement strikers, a centre-half and midfielders who can score goals.

Barry is one of the most envied managers in the country. Got a team problem? – buy a player! No questions asked, no sales needed, the money is on the table. The reason for this is that the ambition of manager and supporters is matched by that of the owners. David and the Golds want success and they will do their bit as owners by finding the money. Barry can never say, if only I had bought him, if only I had the money to do this. There are no excuses anymore. Some say that this puts more pressure on the Manager, and I think that it probably does. But Barry likes it like that, and we are honest and sensible enough to know that spending money in the transfer market does not always guarantee success. Just look at Derby: £12 million spent on players and still in Division One! No, money just increases your chances from nil to possible!

I was asked to arrange pre-season games this year, and I am pleased to say that Barry and I worked together to get Celtic, Liverpool, Manchester United, Sheffield Wednesday, West Bromwich Albion and Chelsea here at St Andrews. The local press and supporters gave us stick about having so many pre-season games, but when you have a squad the size we do you have to play this many games in order to give them all a chance to play. Games are the only way that players get really fit, and in fact the players had about the same number of pre-season games as last year, although the quality of the opposition was a lot higher this time. Before we accept any criticism over the number of games we've played I believe that we should wait and see if the team get off to a good start. Being fit at the start is more important than spending £2 million on new players.

We raised a lot more than the £10,000 we did last year on pre-seasons, but still only enough to pay our ever increasing wage bill for just over two weeks. With all the players we have bought, our annual wage bill is now close to £3,380,000. This is money we have to find before we turn a light bulb on! The season ticket money has gone on players, leaving us to find the money through gate revenue and commercial opportunities to pay this wage. It doesn't look as if I can rely on selling a player to bring money in, having already turned down an offer of £1½ million from Middlesbrough for our captain Liam Daish. Liam is a great captain and would be hard to replace as a player, but even more important is his winning spirit. Plus we have to give Cambridge, the club we bought him from, 17% of any profit over what we paid for him, which was £50,000. When we had the offer for Liam I spoke to Barry and simply asked him, 'Do you want to sell him?' The answer was 'No' and the player is staying. There was no board meeting, no discussion. A simple 'No' from the Manager was all we needed to settle the matter. We want to give ourselves every opportunity of going up again this year, and that means hanging on to your best players – no matter what.

I am pleased to say that the feud between us and the local press has now come to an end. We had a lively clear-the-air meeting at my office with the *Evening Mail*'s Editor Ian Dowell, Managing Director Earnest Petrie and Circulation Director Neil Jagger and actually realized that we are all on the same side. We want only what is best for the football club, and, as the largest local newspaper, so do they. We will never agree on everything, but at least now we have a right of reply and the reporters do actually ring us for our comments before going to press. It has taken a large weight off my mind that we are all now friendly, because it is extremely stressful having the local newspaper digging away at you at every opportunity. How much better it feels to think of them as allies, helpers, people you can trust. Bringing the situation to a head, calling a truce and working together to achieve more has really helped us locally. I now understand more of what the media are all about, and I think that my own personality and career are beginning to be better understood though the pages of the press. Yes, I am still called glamorous, sexy, a stunner and all that by some in the media – which incidentally I am flattered by! – but now when I am asked to give interviews it is not just by male chauvinists chasing a story because I am a woman: now they seek my opinion on commercial, financial and sponsorship matters. It is probably as a consequence of this new portrayal that I have been invited to join the new Football League Commercial Steering Group.

The business of football is like no other, in that you have no competition. Someone who is a Blues supporter will never support Villa, and vice versa, all the way down the line. There is no reason for football clubs not to swap ideas and pass information around freely, but we don't do it enough. We promoted the Auto Windscreen competition very successfully, broke all the attendance records and sold out Wembley. We should pass the marketing plans of this on to the clubs currently in the competition. It is easier to pass on winning ideas than to look for them. By swapping good marketing ideas, new sponsorship opportunities and commercial angles we can all learn, yet we were not doing it. Now the League have set up the Steering Group, and I, along with colleagues at Leicester, Wolves, Crystal Palace, Sheffield United and Walsall, will be exploring new ideas, swapping the best of our own ideas and feeding these into other League clubs. To be recognized as one of the most successful marketing clubs in the Football League is a great honour, and goes a long way to proving that the times are changing and that I am now being seen as a Managing Director rather than a woman.

As my relationship with Barry has improved, so has my relationship with the players. They too have overcome the 'them and us' attitude that made relations strained though last season. They are aware of our commitment to them as individuals as well as parts of a team. We always do our best to make each one happy – normally this means giving them new contracts! – but we are always the first to recognize when a player is on low wages and playing well. We may not always agree on what sort of increase the player gets, but despite sometimes hostile negotiation the players seem to get what they want, within reason.

It is vital to this club that we do well, get into the play-offs or even, God willing, go straight up to the Premiership. There is such a thin line between success and defeat, mostly due to confidence, and Barry certainly inspires that in the players. We desperately need the players we have bought to come right on the field. Most are on two-year contracts and will be virtually impossible to transfer, even on loan, given the high wages they receive from us. It is therefore vital that we do well each season, at least keeping in the top half, so that the gates remain high and the wages can be paid. That is what this season is all about, getting there or thereabouts to keep the dream alive. Our fixture list has arrived and we know that we will be playing Ipswich and Norwich, both relegated from the Premier League last season, in our first two home games. This will be an early test for us, but only time will tell if we bought the right players, did the correct pre-season training and did well to give Barry his three-year contract.

Pre-season has gone well, and things are looking good. Paul Tait's hearing for bringing the game into disrepute after he wore his insulting T-shirt at Wembley went equally well. He received a £500 fine and a severe reprimand from the Football Association, but thankfully no ban. There have been a few ups and downs. Liam Daish, helped by his agent Eric Hall, received a new three-year contract, despite having two years of his current one to run. And I got married.

That was a fabulous day. Great weather and a great turn-out helped make it one of the most special days in my life. My board of directors, the Manager and some of the players from all over the country helped Paul and me to celebrate our big day. It was one of the best weddings I have ever been to! The Dorchester Hotel was a fantastic venue, and every last detail turned out perfectly. I had had nothing at all to do with the wedding, which for most of the year was the furthest thing from my mind. With Wembley, the championship and the baby to think about, arrangements for menus, flowers and invitations were not exactly top priority for me. My mother, who has all too often been forgotten by me – in interviews and in this book – worked incredibly hard to make this day so wonderful. My mother's influence on me is not always apparent, as I take after my father in so many obvious ways. But we are close and I trust her and she is always right!

Three weeks into the 1995–96 season, we have won all our home games, and have won two and lost two away from home. The most recent game, a 5–0 victory at Barnsley (it would have been 6–0 if we had not missed a penalty in the last minute), has given us the confidence to predict great things this season. The dream is becoming reality as each match passes. We are playing good football and we look strong and confident on the ball. When we lose we can't help feeling angry, because during each game it seems as if we can win. This is a feeling I have not had before, because in seasons past when we went ahead we would be praying to hang on and not get beaten. The disaster of Swindon two seasons ago, when we were 4–1 up and lost 6–4, could not be shaken off until now. We are confident that this is going to be a good season for the club. We will be there or thereabouts. We are in the Anglo Italian Cup, hoping to break more attendance records and then go back to a sell-out crowd at Wembley. Only time will tell how the club's fortunes develop this year.

Season **1994/95**
Results

Aug 13	Leyton Orient	away	1–2	Claridge
Aug 16	Shrewsbury	away	1–2	Daish
	Coca-Cola Cup 1st rd (1)			
Aug 20	Chester	home	1–0	Donowa
Aug 23	Shrewsbury	home	2–0	Claridge, Saville
	Coca-Cola Cup 1st rd (2)			
Aug 27	Swansea	away	2–0	Claridge 2
Aug 30	Wycombe	home	0–1	
Sep 3	Plymouth	home	4–2	Regis 2, Tait, Wallace
Sep 10	Oxford Utd	away	1–1	Claridge
Sep 13	Rotherham	away	1–1	Bull
Sep 18	Peterborough	home	4–0	Bull 2, Tait, Dominguez
Sep 20	Blackburn	away	0–2	
	Coca-Cola Cup 2nd rd (1)			
Sep 24	Hull	home	2–2	Claridge, Dominguez
Sep 27	Peterborough	away	5–3	Hunt 3, Bull, Dominguez
Oct 1	Wrexham	away	1–1	Claridge
Oct 4	Blackburn	home	1–1	McGavin
	Coca-Cola Cup 2nd rd (2)			
Oct 8	Huddersfield	home	1–1	Bull
Oct 15	Brighton	away	1–0	Donowa
Oct 18	Walsall	home	3–0	Donowa, Shearer 2
Oct 22	Brentford	away	2–1	Ward, Shearer
Oct 29	Bristol Rovers	home	2–0	Claridge, Bull

Nov 1	Crewe	home	4–0	Hunt 3, Claridge
Nov 5	Shrewsbury	away	2–0	Hunt, Bull
Nov 12	Slough	home	4–0	McGavin 2, Shearer 2
	FA Cup 1st rd			
Nov 19	Bournemouth	home	0–0	
Nov 26	Stockport	away	1–0	Hunt
Nov 29	Gillingham	home	3–0	Poole, McGavin, Tait
Dec 2	Scunthorpe	home	0–0	
	FA Cup 2nd rd			
Dec 10	Chester	away	4–0	Daish, Claridge, McGavin, Lowe
Dec 14	Scunthorpe	away	2–1	Cooper, McGavin
	FA Cup 2nd rd replay			
Dec 17	Leyton Orient	home	2–0	Donowa 2
Dec 26	Cambridge	home	1–1	Otto
Dec 28	Cardiff	away	1–0	Otto
Dec 31	Blackpool	home	7–1	Donowa 2, Claridge 2, Lowe, Parris
Jan 2	Bradford	away	1–1	Cooper
Jan 7	Liverpool	home	0–0	
	FA Cup 3rd rd			
Jan 10	Hereford	home	3–1	Ward, Claridge, Otto
Jan 14	York	away	0–2	
Jan 18	Liverpool	away	1–1	Otto
	FA Cup 3rd rd replay			
Jan 31	Swansea	home	3–2	Claridge, Francis, Tait
	Auto Windscreen semi-final			
Feb 4	Stockport	home	1–0	

Feb 11	Crewe	away	1–0	Donowa
Feb 18	York	home	4–2	Francis 2, Otto, Shearer
Feb 21	Bournemouth	away	1–2	Francis
Feb 25	Wrexham	home	5–2	Donowa, Francis 2, Shearer, Otto
Feb 28	Leyton Orient	home	1–0	Shearer
Mar 4	Hull	away	0–0	
Mar 11	Swansea	home	0–1	
Mar 14	Leyton Orient	away	3–2	Claridge 2, Williams
Mar 18	Wycombe	away	3–0	Claridge, Shearer, Poole
Mar 21	Oxford Utd	home	3–0	Daish, Claridge, Francis
Mar 25	Peterborough	away	1–1	Shearer
Mar 29	Bristol Rovers	away	1–1	Claridge
Apr 1	Rotherham	home	2–1	Francis, Shearer
Apr 4	Blackpool	away	1–1	Claridge
Apr 11	Shrewsbury	home	2–0	Claridge 2
Apr 15	Cardiff	home	2–1	Ward, Tait
Apr 17	Cambridge	away	0–1	
Apr 19	Plymouth	away	3–1	Whyte, Claridge 2
Apr 23	Carlisle	Wembley	1–0	Tait
	Auto Windscreen final			
Apr 26	Brentford	home	2–0	Francis, Daish
Apr 29	Brighton	home	3–3	Ward, Dominguez, Shearer
May 2	Bradford	home	0–0	
May 6	Huddersfield	away	2–1	Claridge, Tait

Season **1995/96**
Fixtures

Aug 12	Ipswich Town	home
Aug 15	Plymouth Argyle	home
	Coca-Cola Cup 1st rd (1)	
Aug 19	Charlton Athletic	away
Aug 22	Plymouth Argyle	away
	Coca-Cola Cup 1st rd (2)	
Aug 26	Norwich City	home
Aug 30	Huddersfield Town	away
Sep 2	Barnsley	away
Sep 5	Genoa	home
	Anglo Italian Group Match	
Sep 9	Crystal Palace	home
Sep 12	Stoke City	home
Sep 17	West Bromwich Albion	away
Sep 23	Watford	away
Sep 30	Oldham Athletic	home
Oct 7	Southend United	home
Oct 11	Perugia	away
	Anglo Italian Group Match	
Oct 14	Portsmouth	away
Oct 21	Grimsby Town	home
Oct 28	Port Vale	away
Nov 4	Millwall	home

Nov 8	Ancona	away
	Anglo Italian Group Match	
Nov 11	Reading	away
Nov 18	Luton Town	away
Nov 21	Derby County	home
Nov 25	Leicester City	home
Dec 2	Southend United	away
Dec 9	Watford	home
Dec 13	Cesena	home
	Anglo Italian Group Match	
Dec 16	Oldham Athletic	away
Dec 23	Tranmere Rovers	home
Dec 26	Sheffield United	away
Dec 30	Sunderland	away
Jan 1	Wolverhampton Wanderers	home
Jan 13	Charlton Athletic	home
Jan 20	Ipswich Town	away
Feb 3	Norwich City	away
Feb 10	Huddersfield	home
Feb 17	Stoke City	away
Feb 20	Barnsley	home
Feb 24	West Bromwich Albion	home
Feb 27	Crystal Palace	away
Mar 2	Sheffield United	home
Mar 9	Tranmere Rovers	away
Mar 16	Sunderland	home
Mar 23	Wolverhampton Wanderers	away

Mar 30	Grimsby Town	away
Apr 2	Portsmouth	home
Apr 6	Port Vale	away
Apr 10	Millwall	away
Apr 13	Luton Town	home
Apr 20	Derby County	away
Apr 27	Leicester City	away
May 4	Reading	home

A brief history of the Blues

Like so many football clubs that started in the late nineteenth century, Birmingham City's origins lie in the Church. The Blues came into being under the name of Small Heath Alliance in 1875, formed by a group of cricketers from Holy Trinity Church in Bordesley Green. In 1877 the club moved to its first ground, Muntz Street, which was rented from the Gressey family for £5 a year! On 27 September 1879, the 'Heathens' had an engagement at Muntz Street which was to form the beginnings of that great Midlands rivalry with Aston Villa. Small Heath won the game by a margin recorded as 'one goal and a disputed goal to nil'! The club turned professional in 1885, striking an agreement with the players whereby they received half of the gate money. In 1888 the Blues became the first club to adopt limited liability – its share capital was £650! In

1905 the club changed its name from Small Heath Alliance to Birmingham Football Club.

By now the club's growth meant that a change of ground was necessary. The Blues moved to the current St Andrews site in 1906, and the first game at St Andrews was played against Middlesbrough in December of that year in front of a crowd of 32,000. Sir John Holder kicked off the match and the first game finished goalless. The first goal at St Andrews was scored three days later by Benny Green, who was rewarded with a piano for his efforts – legend has it that Benny had already found a buyer for the instrument. He had to be 'thawed out' after his goal as he threw himself into a pile of snow while in the act of scoring.

During the First World War the Blues were asked to help the cause by offering the use of St Andrews as a rifle range to train soldiers. In the 1920–21 season the club did not enter the FA Cup competition – secretary Sam Richards simply forgot to send the forms in! The 1925–26 season saw the first visit to St Andrews by foreign opposition when Real Madrid were beaten 3–0 in a friendly. In 1931 the Blues graced Wembley for the first time, playing against West Brom in the FA Cup final, which they lost 2–1 after a great game. The following year saw the Blues attract the highest ever attendance at St Andrews, with 67,341 people turning out to watch an FA Cup tie against Everton. Manager George Liddell (1933–39) used no fewer than seventy players during his six years at the helm. Between 1920 and 1935 Joe Bradford, the club's all time record goalscorer, amassed 267 goals in 445 appearances. Bradford won twelve England caps, scoring seven goals.

In the Second World War the club paid a high price, losing both the Railway End and the Main Stand. The Spion Kop roof fell down and the ground was in a sorry state. The German Luftwaffe scored no fewer than twenty direct hits on the ground during the war years. This led to all home games being played at Villa Park. When the move back to St Andrews became possible in 1943, the players had to change in a nearby factory. A massive clean-up operation was launched and an apple tree was found to be growing through debris on the Kop.

The 1946 season was one of the club's most successful to date, with the winning of the Football League Championship and an FA Cup semi-final appearance. In the three seasons after the war the Blues were not far short of being invincible: they were beaten only eight times at home in 63 matches. They conceded only 102 goals in 126 League games and they won the Second Division title in 1947–48. The 1954–55 season saw the Blues, under Arthur Turner, gain promotion from the Second to the First Division. They clinched the Second Division title on the last day of the season, edging Luton into second spot and taking the title by 0.297 of a goal. Turner had one of the best sides ever to play at St Andrews, and during that promotion season they scored 92 League goals with all of the front four reaching double figures. In 1956 Blues had their best season to date in the First Division, finishing in sixth place and reaching the FA Cup final. In 1960 Birmingham City become the first English club to play in Europe and reached the Fairs Cup final, losing to Barcelona 1–4 on aggregate. The Blues' FA Cup tie with Bury in season 1962–63 was postponed no fewer than fourteen times. There was also one abandonment and a replay, making a total of sixteen attempts before it was decided!

In 1970 Trevor Francis made his first appearance for the club. He became a Blues legend, scoring 133 goals in 328 appearances. Nine years later he became the first £1 million English footballer when he moved to Nottingham Forest. In 1972 the club gained promotion to the First Division and reached the FA Cup semi-finals. The 1970s was a period of stability in the top flight. Another of the great teams to have played at St Andrews enjoyed seven seasons in Division One. The only player to appear for Birmingham City with a World Cup winner's medal to his name was the Argentinian, Alberto Tarantini, who helped his country lift the star prize in 1978. The Blues have also had a manager who gained a World Cup winner's medal in Sir Alf Ramsey, who managed the club in 1977–78. The bubble burst in 1979 with the Blues being relegated to Division Two. When Blues keeper Tony Coton, 19, made his League debut on 27 December 1980, his first touch of the ball was to save a penalty after just 85 seconds against Sunderland. The Blues won the game 3–2.

A yo-yo period followed, with the Blues gaining promotion the next year and then being relegated to the Second Division in 1984. The following season we were promoted back to the First Division, only to be relegated again. In 1989 things went from bad to worse as the Blues were relegated to the Third Division for the first time in their history. In 1992 the club became the first team to be promoted from the Third to the First Division as the divisions were restructured. The arrival of David Sullivan and the Gold brothers in April 1993 led to a period of financial stability, and under the managerial reigns of Terry Cooper, and with a much needed cash injection on the playing side, the club escaped almost certain relegation. Paul Moulden, a signing from Oldham Athletic, scored a last gasp winner in the last game of the season against Charlton to ensure that the Blues would be playing First Division football the next season. The 1993–94 season saw the Blues struggle in the First Division. A managerial change, with Barry Fry replacing Terry Cooper, and more cash could not stave off the beckoning Second Division. Bulldozers moved in on the Spion Kop and Tilton Road ends after the game against Bristol City on Saturday 16 April. A new £10 million development was started to replace the famous old terracing. The Blues were relegated in May 1994 after a spirited fight.

The 1994–95 season was a success for the Blues, even though plying their trade in the Second Division. Two exciting cup encounters against Blackburn and Liverpool proved the team's championship credentials, with Birmingham losing 3–1 over two legs in the Coca-Cola Cup to Blackburn (who went on to win the Premiership), and after a replay against Liverpool in the FA Cup the Blues lost out on penalties. In December of that year the club smashed their record paid transfer fee by paying £800,000 for Southend's Ricky Otto, and then a month later equalled it by paying Stockport the same amount for Kevin Francis. These two signings boosted the club's championship push, and on Saturday 6 May the Blues were crowned Second Division Champions after beating Huddersfield 2–1 with goals from Steve Claridge and Paul Tait. The Auto Windscreen Shield competition drew record crowds with attendances of over 20,000 for the latter rounds of the competition. The Blues went on to win the trophy in a Wembley final that attracted a sell-out 76,663 crowd. In June 1995 the Blues sold José Dominguez to Sporting Lisbon for a club record received transfer fee of £1.5 million, beating the previous record of £1 million when Trevor Francis moved to Nottingham Forest in 1979.